On Extinction

On Extinction

Beginning Again at the End

Ben Ware

VERSO

London • New York

First published by Verso 2024
© Ben Ware 2024

1 3 5 7 9 10 8 6 4 2

Verso
UK: 6 Meard Street, London W1F 0EG
US: 388 Atlantic Avenue, Brooklyn, NY 11217
versobooks.com

Verso is the imprint of New Left Books

ISBN-13: 978-1-78873-999-3
ISBN-13: 978-1-83976-067-9 (UK EBK)
ISBN-13: 978-1-83976-068-6 (US EBK)

British Library Cataloguing in Publication Data
A catalogue record for this book is available from the British Library

Library of Congress Cataloging-in-Publication Data
A catalog record for this book is available
from the Library of Congress

Typeset in Sabon by Biblichor Ltd, Scotland
Printed and bound by CPI Group (UK) Ltd, Croydon CR0 4YY

For Sarah – again, and again

It's the end that is the worst, then the middle, then the end,
in the end it's the end that is the worst.

Samuel Beckett, *The Unnamable*

Contents

Preface

I.

To talk about extinction is to talk about an end: a disappearance, a vanishing, a blotting out. But ends, even apparently final ones, are rarely straightforward.

In 'The Burial of the Dead', the first part of T. S. Eliot's 1922 poem *The Waste Land*, we encounter the following lines:

> Unreal City,
> Under the brown fog of a winter dawn,
> A crowd flowed over London Bridge, so many,
> I had not thought death had undone so many.

Eliot's 'Unreal City' is often read as an evocation of London reeling from the shock and horror of World War I. Equally plausibly, however, it might be read as a city traumatized ('undone') by the influenza pandemic of 1918, when the burial of the dead became so overwhelming that undertakers ran out of coffins and families had to bury their loved ones in back gardens. As one of the speakers in Eliot's poem goes on to ask:

> That corpse you planted last year in your garden,
> Has it begun to sprout? Will it bloom this year?
> Or has the sudden frost disturbed its bed?

I was reminded of Eliot's words during the first Covid lockdown of 2020, amid the still-unfolding nightmare of distancing, disease, and death. Who, at such a moment, could prevent their thoughts from turning – and anxiously returning – to ideas of transience, finitude, and, ultimately, extinction? But at the same time the virus also hinted at another kind of ending: the end of the current social arrangement and the emergence of something new. *Surely things can't simply revert back to the old ways after all this? Surely new things will grow out of the wasteland!*

The pandemic, however, as we now see, left us 'undone' not just by what it delivered, but also by what it failed to deliver. While millions lost their lives, the system did not budge an inch: the fantasy of Covid as the end that would 'change everything' – an end that would end all of our previous failed endings – turned out to be naively optimistic. Indeed, what the so-called 'corona apocalypse' ultimately unveiled was not a big spectacular ending, but precisely the opposite: the end as one long emergency *without end*; the end as an undying present that remains forever sick.

This exhausted situation is where we find ourselves today. But being stuck at the end is clearly not just a consequence of the pandemic. We also face a number of other ends, and possible worse ends to come: climate and ecological catastrophe, new geo-political conflicts, accelerating economic and social chaos. Like the characters in Samuel Beckett's play *Endgame*, we appear to inhabit a historical moment when everything is (or at least seems to be) on its way to becoming 'finished', 'corpsed'. But the question that *Endgame* only ever hints at is precisely the one that this book places front and centre: how might we imagine a future that is not simply an extension of the blighted present? What will it mean – both philosophically and politically speaking – to *begin again at the end*?

II.

On Extinction does not provide another commentary on what has come to be known as the sixth mass extinction; nor does it examine, in scientific detail, issues of climate change and habitat loss. Rather, the book is, first and foremost, a philosophical and psychoanalytic critique of our damaged times. It deals with the converging catastrophes of the present (ecological, geo-political, social), but it does so by drawing them into a fresh narrative. Advancing in a modernist spirit, the book presents the reader with a series of new conjunctions: Kant's 'The End of All Things' alongside Brecht's excremental vision of capitalist culture; the Marquis de Sade and contemporary warfare; Kafka as a critic of bourgeois environmentalism; Freud unwittingly entangled in a cluster of contemporary debates ranging from anti-natalism to de-extinction. And all of this just for starters . . . or perhaps for endings.

The book's basic wager is that it is only by seeing our crisis-ridden present from sideways on – through the 'distorting' lens of philosophy and culture – that we can come to see it clearly and thus discover new openings for political thought and action.

In tarrying with various kinds of endings, however, the book inevitably encounters the question of time – something which today assumes a strange logic. On the one hand, we are told that it is already 'too late': we have missed our moment to act, time has effectively run out, and there is now nothing to be done. On the other hand, we hear that there is still time but it's disappearing fast: we must therefore act and '*act now*' in order to forestall an imminent disaster. These two senses of time correspond to two different modes of enjoyment (or, in psychoanalytic terms, two different modes of *jouissance*). In the first case, what is enjoyed is the idea of catastrophe itself, along with our own assumed guilt: everything is already over and it is 'we' ('humanity' as a whole) who are responsible. In the second case, what is enjoyed is the sense of anxious urgency, coupled with the belief that we are now tasked with 'saving' the planet. While 'too late' leads in the direction of melancholic inaction, 'act now' initiates various forms of narcissistic hyperactivity.

As the book makes clear, we need to take time to think again about time. Beyond narratives centred around dooms-day clocks, tipping points, and climate deadlines we need to ask how we might emancipate time, how a new sense of collective time can be made to appear. It is not that we are out of time, or that time has almost run out – both of these positions might be read as symptoms of the fact that we find ourselves in an expanding present that has been stripped of any real sense of the future or the past. Rather than today's crisis time, what is required is a new form of politics allied to a dialectical sense of time. This will be a politics of the future that strives towards what Marx calls *the conscious completion of old work*: the actualization of the radical past through its repetition and fulfilment in the here and now. Such a politics is certainly untimely; but it's the only point from which to begin.

A Dialectics of Extinction

The End

I.

In his late essay 'The End of All Things', Immanuel Kant walks us towards the edge of a mental abyss. He invites us to imagine a scenario in which 'the whole of nature will be rigid and as it were petrified: the last thought, the last feeling in the thinking subject will then stop and remain forever the same without any change'.[1] This idea of an absolute end is both 'horrifying' and 'attractive': 'frighteningly sublime', as Kant puts it. While such an end, strictly speaking, cannot be thought (it implies 'an end of all time', which we are unable to cognize), it is certainly not a meaningless idea. For Kant, the moral perfection that humans aspire towards cannot be realized within time, marked as it is by a constant alteration of their moral and physical state. This leads to the idea of a *final end*, which (at the same time) is the beginning of a duration in which beings as *supersensible* no longer stand under conditions of time and in which their ultimate moral end can thus be attained. The idea of an end of all things is therefore what gives worth to the world of rational beings; without it, as Kant writes, 'creation itself appears purposeless ... like a play having no resolution and affording no cognition of any rational aim'.

The idea of a final end is, for Kant, an idea of 'reason'; but thinking about it inevitably becomes a kind of *repetition compulsion.* As he says, we 'cannot cease' turning our 'terrified gaze back to [it] again and again'. This latter point is true with respect to both philosophy and contemporary culture. In the case of philosophy, thought is, we might say, forever haunted and fascinated by the possibility of extinction, wipeout, and ultimately its own negation. Nietzsche's *oeuvre*, to take just one example, begins with (the fantasy of) an end. At the start of his posthumously published fragment 'On the Truth and Lies in a Nonmoral Sense', we encounter the following fable:

> Once upon a time, in some out of the way corner of that universe which is dispersed into numberless twinkling solar systems, there was a star upon which clever beasts invented knowing. That was the most arrogant and mendacious minute of 'world history', but nevertheless, it was only a minute. After nature had drawn a few breaths, the star cooled and congealed, and the clever beasts had to die. – One might invent such a fable, and yet he still would not have adequately illustrated how miserable, how shadowy and transient, how aimless and arbitrary the human intellect looks within nature. There were eternities during which it did not exist. And when it is all over with the human intellect, nothing will have happened.[2]

Writing in the shadow of the Paris Commune, which he took to be an apocalyptic event, Nietzsche here imagines the extinction of all human life in a heat-death scenario.[3] While the author's tone is both provocative and playful, it is nevertheless possible to read the fable as enacting a double philosophical-ideological move. First, a refutation of the revolutionary project as such: occupying a minute position within the universe, the human species is a 'miserable', 'aimless', and ultimately insignificant thing, and from this cosmological perspective all political change becomes meaningless. And second, a critique of the anthropocentric worldview: consumed by 'arrogance', human beings see themselves as separate from other natural beings, as occupying a privileged place, believing, in Nietzsche's words, that 'the eyes of the universe are telescopically focused' upon them.

This sets up an interesting confrontation with Kant. In 'The End of All Things', the idea of a final end is implicitly tied to the belief that the world exists for the sake of its rational inhabitants. And indeed, when Kant goes on to speak about the expectation of a *terrible end* to come – a cosmic catastrophe delivered as divine punishment for the 'corruption' of the species – this further expresses a conviction that humans are in some sense exceptional in the order of world-beings. While Nietzsche's critique of anthropocentrism might, by contrast, appear progressive, striking a chord with a certain strand of contemporary ecological thought, we should nevertheless bear in mind that this critique emerges directly from the philosopher's anti-collectivist, anti-revolutionary position. It is, in fact, a profound aversion to the radical human rights proclaimed by the French Revolution – and later by the Communards – that stimulates Nietzsche's rejection of anthropocentrism.[4] What is more, while this critique stresses the continuity between human beings and the rest of nature, it also emphasizes what it takes to be the vast differences among human beings themselves – the 'slave' versus the 'master', the 'lumpen' versus the '*Übermensch*', the 'Semite' versus the 'Aryan' – and, in this respect, it can be seen as a direct precursor of modern forms of eco-fascism.

To the extent that it grounds fantasies of conquest and divine entitlement, a certain idea of human exceptionalism should of course be resolutely rejected. At the same time, however, we need to be mindful of the ways in which liberal-philosophical arguments against anthropocentrism often obscure and exacerbate the very problems which they purport to solve. Such arguments have become increasingly common in our own period of terrible ends: an era of accelerating climate change, ecological depredation, and the spectre of mass extinction. In an article for *Time* magazine, for example, Judith Butler makes the following claim:

> An inhabitable world for humans depends on a flourishing earth that does not have humans at its center. We oppose environmental toxins not only so that we humans can live and breathe without fear of being poisoned, but also because the water and the air must have lives that are not centered on our own. As we dismantle the rigid forms of individuality in these interconnected times, we can imagine the smaller part that human worlds must play on this earth whose regeneration we depend upon – and which, in turn, depends upon our smaller and more mindful role.[5]

Here human exceptionalism is paradoxically affirmed at the very point at which it is rejected. Humans, we are told, must radically de-centre themselves with respect to the earth; dismantle all hitherto existing ontological hierarchies; and fold themselves modestly into the great interconnected network of animate and inanimate things. But these moral injunctions serve only to *foreground the human*. First, and mostly obviously, the idea of a new relation to the earth is one that makes sense only from the human standpoint: it is a human-all-too-human fantasy, towards which the earth and nature remain utterly indifferent. In this respect, we might say that the *eco* is, in typically anthropocentric fashion, wholly consumed by the philosophical *ego*.

Second, the notion of an 'inhabitable world', as it is here presented, might be read as a point of convergence between liberal environmentalism and a strange kind of eco-political disavowal. At precisely the moment when collective and large-scale human interventions are called for, we hear instead that the future depends upon humans adopting a 'smaller and more mindful role', in order to create an environment free of 'toxins' in which air and water acquire their own distinctive and dynamic agency.[6] But this, once again, is a uniquely human vision: one falling somewhere between deep ecology, New Age animism, and a Disney cartoon fantasy.

One of the main problems with liberal anti-anthropocentricism is not so much that the human (unwittingly) re-emerges centre stage, but that it does so in exactly the wrong kind of way. Rather than the fiction of a chastened humanity treading lightly on the earth and achieving some kind of harmonious 'balance' with nature, we need to begin instead by acknowledging that human beings are in fact *freaks of nature*: constitutively divided speaking beings; subjects of the unconscious and the death drive; and beings who are dialectical contradictions – on the one hand, part of nature (emerging immanently out of it) and, on the other hand, standing apart from this very nature (acquiring a degree of independence and autonomy from it). This latter point is crucial and can be further developed along lines suggested by Hegel and a number of his contemporary psychoanalytic interlocutors.

The subject that emerges from nature, and which separates itself off from nature in order to achieve a kind of self-relating independence, is, we might say, an effect of the *non-identity at the heart of nature*, the failure of nature to be fully natural. As Adrian Johnston remarks, nature is not some 'placid organic evenness . . . undisturbed by any destabilizing imbalances'; rather it is *'perturbed from within itself'*.[7] The subject is thus the name of the fissure by way of which nature becomes 'alien' to itself;[8] it is the push of natural substance to produce its own otherness; and this, at least in one respect, is what Hegel means when he says that 'substance shows itself to be essentially subject'.[9] Putting the point slightly differently and adapting a phrase from Jacques Lacan, we can say that there is something in nature *more than nature itself*; and this extra something, this *exteriority* which is also *interior*, is the human subject which nature generates out of itself.[10]

But to think of the subject as dialectically entwined with nature is also to think of nature as *ontologically incomplete*: as having a void or hole inscribed at its very centre. 'At the level of nature', as Althusser writes, the human subject 'is an absurdity, a gap in being, an "empty nothing," a "night"' – the final references here being to Hegel's 1805–6 *Jenaer Realphilosophe* manuscript, and to his famous description of human beings as 'the night of the world'.[11] This empty nothing, this void of pure negativity which *is* the subject, operates however in a powerfully double sense: it is both *the wound of nature*, the rupturing of any unified identity that substance might have enjoyed with itself, and simultaneously the attempt to *heal the wound* by constructing a universe of meaning out of negativity itself.[12] If we are to think the relation between subject and nature, then it is from this point that we need to begin: first, with the subject as nature's inner disturbance, its excess of negativity, that which prevents it from achieving any kind of harmonious internal 'balance'; and second, with the experience of negativity itself (including an awareness of our *non-rapport* with nature) as the very precondition for the appearance of a new kind of human universality which can make possible a transformed relationship with all living things.[13]

II.

How then might we locate the historical origin of the kind of subject we have here been describing? Out of what sort of world does this subject emerge? While Hegel has one kind of answer to these questions, here we can close the circle and turn instead to a footnote in 'The End of All Things' where the Sage of Königsberg provides us with another kind of answer. Drawing on the work of a certain 'Persian wit', Kant says that 'our earthly world', the dwelling place of the human subject, originated as a '*cloaca*' – a shit house – 'where all the excrement from the other worlds [was] deposited'. According to this account, in paradise, the dwelling place of the first human couple,

there was a garden with ample trees richly provided with splendid fruits, whose digested residue, after the couple's enjoyment of them, vanished through an unnoticed evaporation; the exception was a single tree in the middle of the garden, which bore a fruit which was delicious but did not dry up in this way. As it now happened, our first parents now lusted after it, despite the prohibition against tasting it, and so there was no other way to keep heaven from being polluted except to take the advice of one of the angels who pointed out to them the distant earth, with the words: 'There is the toilet of the whole universe,' and then carried them there in order to relieve themselves, but then flew back to heaven leaving them behind. This is how the human race [arose] on earth.[14]

This scatological re-telling of the myth of the Fall proves to be extremely useful. First, as Kant elsewhere suggests, the eating of the fruit is not a moral crime, but rather an originary *liberation from nature*.[15] The Fall, in this respect, is nothing other than a fall *into subjectivity* – an act of radical self-positing at which point the aforementioned ontological crack in nature appears. Second, from the contemporary perspective, we can take Kant's footnote as a reminder that there can be no return to a paradisical world completely free of 'toxins', 'emissions', and 'pollution'. Our world is a world of waste: a mountain of shit, piling ever skywards, which now includes not just human effluence, but also carbon dioxide, methane, plastics, asbestos, heavy metals, deadly chemicals, radioactive material, and trashed electronics. Not to mention endless digital spam, masses of obsolete data stored in the cloud, and the daily churn of social media trash. '*Civilization is the sewer*', as Lacan writes in a late essay,[16] a remark which we might read here as saying not only that civilization emerges with the invention of sewage systems, but also that our own 'civilization' has now become *nothing but a sewer* – a gigantic mansion built out of crap, to paraphrase Bertolt Brecht's memorable line.[17]

Varieties of the End

I.

If modern philosophy can't stop returning to the idea of the end, then the same is also true of contemporary culture. Within culture, however, the fantasy of the end takes a number of distinct forms which we will need to be theoretically attentive to.

In the 2021 film *How It Ends*, the central character Liza (Zoe Lister-Jones) navigates her last day on Earth. Sporting an inconspicuous Chanel leather backpack, and with her younger self (her 'metaphysical YS') in tow, Liza walks the streets of suburban Los Angeles attempting to settle accounts with her parents, friends, and various ex-lovers, before a life-destroying meteorite finally strikes the earth. The impending prospect of mass extinction is here a breezy affair, involving breakfast pancakes, psychedelic drugs, and a sentimental singalong with the indie-folk performer Sharon Van Etten. In this version of world-destroying catastrophe, there is no social breakdown, no struggles over access to resources, and no tooled-up military personnel patrolling the streets. Indeed, the film's key ideological manoeuvre is to displace all evil from *inside* the world (capitalist economic and social relations) to *outside* (the chaotic universe itself), while at the same time presenting annihilation as part of the mildly eccentric everyday run of things. The end is, consequently, not only something over which the characters have no control, but also something which they can *enjoy* as pure unadulterated spectacle.

We might refer to this particular fantasy of the end as the *end as sublime event* – that is, the end as spectacular catastrophe, an abrupt and violent intrusion arriving from elsewhere. The idea of the end as involving a total destruction of the earth can best be grasped, at least in our own period, in the context of a broader ideological shift that occurs at the end of the Cold War. This shift is emblematized in Francis Fukuyama's infamous thesis that world history has reached its categorical conclusion since there is no longer any viable alternative to Western liberal capitalism.[18] Rather than signalling a final end, however, what this argument announces is precisely the opposite: the impossibility of an end, and specifically the impossibility of ending capitalism or of capitalism as we know it ever coming to an end. This, as

Alenka Zupančič points out, plays a crucial role in restructuring the limits of political thought and imagination: 'the end, or any kind of serious transformation', can now only be conceived of as coming catastrophically 'from the great *Outside*'.[19]

We can, however, add a double dialectical twist to this argument. The fantasy of a world-destroying end might be seen to operate in a curiously twofold sense. First, this fantasy functions as a kind of psychic defence: the idea of a sublime ending provides a protective shield against the real horror that history no longer has any aim or purpose, meaning that we might now have arrived at something like a new *chronic mode*, which may well be a state infinitely worse than death.[20] Second, rather than signalling capitalism's (Fukuyamist) triumph, the fantasy of a final end is, we might say, an effect of an internal disturbance within capitalism itself. As George Caffentzis writes: 'whenever the ongoing model of exploitation becomes untenable, capital has intimations of mortality *qua* the world's end'.[21] But because there is never anything secure about the capitalist model, this apocalyptic fear becomes part of capitalism's own chronic condition: *the fantasy of capital is inseparable from the anxiety about the apocalypse of capital.*

Taking the two points together, we thus arrive at an intriguing paradox: the idea of a final end is a defence against the idea that the present state of things will never end; but this is itself a fantasy which conceals the real truth that the spectre of the end is precisely what haunts capitalism. Ultimately, then, we might conclude that the recurrent fantasy of a sublime end has its material basis in capitalism's anxiety about its own ability to reproduce itself over time. It is as if the system secretly knows that it is moving inexorably in the direction of its own extinction.

II.

The fantasy of the end as sublime event can be contrasted with another idea of ending: the end as repetition, as stuckness, an end that seems to play out endlessly.

In Darren Aronofsky's 2019 film *mother!*, a husband and wife live alone in a grand isolated house. The husband (Javier Bardem), named 'Him', is a poet struggling to find creative inspiration. His wife (Jennifer Lawrence), the film's unnamed 'mother', is at work carefully restoring the house after (at some previous, unspecified time) it was destroyed in a fire. The uneasy peace between the couple is interrupted only minutes into the film by the arrival of an uninvited guest ('the doctor'), and then, shortly afterwards, by the appearance of his wife. While Him happily accepts the new couple into the house and invites them to stay as long as they wish, mother is perplexed: she isn't consulted on the matter and the bizarre guests clearly have no respect for her home – they smoke indoors, fuck wherever they please, and fill the place with their vomit, trash, and dirty laundry. As the film progresses, and by various shocking twists and turns, more and more strangers arrive at the house, proceeding to completely destroy the environment which mother has created and finally to violate the body of mother herself.

An obvious ecological reading presents itself here: mother is Mother Nature, Gaia, the 'goddess' of Earth; while Him and the host of other characters are exploitative, 'ecophobic' humanity, the destructive *anthropos*. Mother, in her own words, has created a 'paradise', but she and her home (the two are in fact one) are seen only as a resource: they provide the care and nurture which allow Him to 'create' and the setting for the violent and hedonistic enjoyment of the intruders. When mother's child is taken from her and brutally murdered and eaten by the untamed hordes, this, the film unsubtly suggests, is what our relation to nature has now become.

But this ecological reading is precisely the film's ideological trap. To go along with such an account is to find oneself caught up in the various distortions and misrecognitions which frame the film as a whole: humanity is the disease; the earth is over-populated (mother nature's house is now full); given the degraded state into which civilization has now fallen, the only way of protecting mother nature would be by installing some new kind of eco-authoritarian big Other.

It is here, then, that we should attempt to turn the film inside out by means of a number of specific questions. Aren't the intruders themselves part of nature, its perverse inner disturbance, what is in nature more than nature itself? Doesn't the disorder in mother nature's house therefore reveal the catastrophe at the heart of nature, what Lacan calls nature's 'rottenness' (*pouritture*) 'out of which oozes culture as *antiphusis*' (anti-nature)?[22] While the film traffics in the nostalgic idea of a return to primitive conditions, doesn't this fantasy of a return to a state of pre-castrated earthly innocence also turn out to be a masculine fantasy in its purest form: one in which nature figures as both mother and virgin?

But this is not all. The film's suggestion that 'we' – the human species – are all equally responsible for the destruction of the earth is aligned with the thesis of the anthropocene, a thesis that moves simultaneously in two directions: on the one hand, the planet has now entered a new geological era in which the human is the dominant force; on the other hand, precisely because the anthropocene is a new geological epoch, any *real* historical agency on the part of the human species is rendered obsolete.²³ Mastery and impotence thus coincide; and politically and temporally speaking we arrive at a new endless end: an inescapable enclosure, an era of irreversible species alienation in which the past is extinguished and the future occluded. Isn't it *this* empty looped temporality, rather than simply the depredations of nature, which the film dramatizes and seemingly cannot get outside?

At the close of the film, after mother's house has been reduced to ruins, Him reaches into mother's charred body and pulls out a crystal – an *objet a* (an object *cause* of desire²⁴) – that will allow him to go on with his 'work'. The film then cuts to a scene in which a young woman wakes up in bed in the same house – a repetition of one of the film's opening scenes. Is the young woman mother? Yes and no. It is in fact her double (played by a different actor): the whole drama of the end is thus set up to repeat on a potentially endless loop. We are, as the lyrics of the Skeeter Davis outro song suggest, stuck at 'the end of the world' because we have now lost the love of mother nature. And yet, might it not be here, at the moment of closing, that a space also opens up in which the end – and specifically the apparently endless end of our 'anthropocenic' present – can be dialectically re-thought?

III.

The first thing to say here is that the end, at least in certain instances, provides the subject with a way of *going on*. It is not only a cause of anxiety and dread, but also a source of enjoyment. The wild excitement of Him in the face of world destruction is an instance of what we might call *apocalyptic jouissance*.

We can follow this idea into the domain of contemporary eco-activism, where it connects up with the issue of masochism. For Gilles Deleuze, masochism involves a double attitude towards the law: on the one hand, the law is transferred onto the mother and identified with the image of the mother; on the other hand, the masochist carries out a humorous subversion of the law by zealously following it to the letter.[25] In the case of the activist group Extinction Rebellion (XR), however, Deleuze's definition is turned upside down. XR's masochistic acts of self-inflicted pain – locking their bodies onto inanimate objects, sewing their lips together, playing dead, and deliberately attempting to get arrested by the police – have a clear twofold aim. First, they attempt to provoke the anxiety of the other (in this case 'the government'); second, rather than subverting the law, they attempt to call it forth, to bring it fully into being:[26] what is desired is a new Master figure who will acknowledge the activists' 'demands' and integrate them into the law's own functioning through the creation of a 'Citizens' Assembly'.[27]

What is appealed to here, then, is the law of the father, rather than the (Deleuzean) law of the mother; and this return to paternal authority is underscored by Lacan when he rewrites perversion as *père-version*.[28] Paradoxically, however, it is the law's own failure, its refusal to operate in the way that the activist demands, that opens up the space for the latter's *apocalyptic jouissance*: 'climate change: we're fucked', as the infinitely repeated and endlessly enjoyed XR slogan has it – a phrase that in connecting the threat of annihilation with sexual gratification perfectly sums up the political impotence of the contemporary eco-masochist. In striving to bring an end to the threat of the end (the destruction of the planet), eco-masochism merely adds to the prevailing culture of the endless end: Spectacle (of protest), Arrest (by the authorities), Demand (that the capitalist state 'act' and 'tell the truth') – a SAD politics repeated ad infinitum.

And yet, by observing this ideological impasse it is also possible to glimpse a new way forward. Simply put, to break out of the endless end – the anthropocenic end as spirit-devouring empty repetition – we will need to begin by refraining from making the wrong appeals, to the wrong people, at the wrong time. Here Franz Kafka can act as our political guide. His remarkable micro-story 'Give It Up!' (*'Gibs auf!'*), written between 1917 and 1923, and unpublished during the author's lifetime, reads as follows:

> It was very early in the morning, the streets clean and deserted, I was on my way to the station. As I compared the tower clock with my watch I realized that it was much later than I had thought and that I had to hurry; the shock of this discovery made me feel uncertain of the way, I wasn't very well acquainted with the town yet; fortunately, there was a policeman at hand, I ran to him and breathlessly asked him the way. He smiled and said: 'You asking me the way?' 'Yes,' I said, 'since I can't find it myself.' 'Give it up, give it up!', said he, and turned with a sudden jerk, like someone who wants to be alone with his laughter.[29]

In Kafka's tale, the figure of authority being appealed to for help is one whose function it is to preserve existing social and economic relations, and one who is therefore incapable of providing any kind of direction. Indeed, requesting them do so is enough to raise laughter: 'You want help from me? *Me? Really?* Well, if that's what it has come to, I suggest you give it up!' We should let this stand as Kafka's lesson on the pitfalls of asking those in power (or those whose role it is to serve power) to show us the way out of our current emergency. If the future is to be salvaged and the dead time of the present to be redeemed, it will only be through the transformative agency of those who have learned how to take political sides.

Atomic Philosophy

I.

The philosophical concern with the end is, it would seem, precisely what cannot be ended. The post-Kantian tradition not only announces (and then re-announces) the death of God, man, metaphysics, history, and art; it is also endlessly preoccupied with the death of philosophy as such. Commenting upon the ubiquity of this particular motif, Alain Badiou writes as follows:

> The great declarations concerning the death of philosophy in general, and of metaphysics in particular, are most probably a rhetorical means of introducing a new way, or a new goal, into philosophy itself. The best means of saying: I am a new philosopher, is probably to say: philosophy is finished, philosophy is dead . . . It is not impossible that the development of philosophy must always be in the form of resurrection. The old philosophy, like the old man, is dead, but this death is in fact the birth of the new man, the new philosopher.[30]

For Badiou, the end and the beginning thus coincide: announcing the end of philosophy is a means of clearing the ground, of allowing a new mode of thought – or a new *style* of thought – to emerge out of the ruins of the old. But because the theme of the end continues to play out, the future of philosophy, like its past, can only be understood as a *creative repetition*.[31] Borrowing a useful image from music, Badiou argues that 'the becoming of philosophy has the classical form of the theme and its variations. The repetition provides the theme, and the constant novelty, the variations.'[32]

But here a series of crucial questions also opens up. What happens when certain political conditions threaten to bring repetition itself to an end? What becomes of philosophical thought when the end of all things moves from being a speculative idea to a concrete possibility? If philosophy (as Hegel famously suggests) comes into being when night falls, what occurs when this night, losing its dialectical relationship with light, seems no longer to be a precursor to a new dawn, a new age?

II.

In 1946, Ludwig Wittgenstein makes a startling claim – one that is less a comment on his own philosophical enterprise and more a piece of social and cultural critique:

The hysterical fear of the atom bomb the public now has, or at least expresses, is almost a sign that here for once a really salutary discovery has been made. At least the fear gives the impression of being fear in the face of a really effective bitter medicine. I cannot rid myself of the thought: if there were not something good here, the philistines would not be making an outcry. But perhaps this too is a childish idea. For all I can mean really is that the bomb creates the prospect of the end, the destruction of a ghastly evil, of disgusting soapy water science and certainly that is not an unpleasant thought; but who is to say what would come after such a destruction? The people now making speeches against the production of the bomb are undoubtedly the dregs of the intelligentsia, but even that does not prove beyond question that what they abominate is to be welcomed.[33]

What should we make of these remarks, written almost one year after the US bombings of Hiroshima and Nagasaki – events which left almost a quarter of a million people dead? While the poet Gertrude Stein notes that she 'had not been able to take any interest' in the atomic bomb, Wittgenstein appears deeply invested in it, and for what would seem to be two connected reasons.[34] First, the bomb offers the prospect of an 'end', and specifically the destruction of the 'ghastly evil' that for him is *scientism*. Second, the bomb might be thought of as a welcome invention (an 'effective bitter medicine') precisely because those opposing it (including the likes of Russell and Einstein) are, in Wittgenstein's words, 'philistines', the 'dregs of the intelligentsia'.[35] While Wittgenstein is quick to acknowledge that the latter is perhaps a 'childish idea' (he is simply welcoming what his intellectual opponents are against), his general remarks about the bomb need to be understood in relation to a number of other statements that he makes during the same period. The following remark from 1947 is crucial:

> *The truly apocalyptic view* of the world is that things do *not* repeat themselves. It is not e.g. absurd to believe that the scientific & technological age is the beginning of the end for humanity, that the idea of Great Progress is a bedazzlement, along with the idea that the truth will ultimately be known; that there is nothing good or desirable about scientific knowledge & that humanity, in seeking it, is falling into a trap. It is by no means clear that this is not how things are.[36]

According to Wittgenstein, then, the truly apocalyptic view is one that sees humanity marching directly towards its end (without the chance to repeat, to learn from past mistakes); but this end emerges as a real possibility only with the arrival of the so-called scientific-technological age. In the epoch of 'great progress', in which science becomes the only accepted form of knowledge, humankind sinks (as Wittgenstein puts it elsewhere) into a world of 'infinite misery', into a new 'darkness', in which 'peace is the last thing that will find a home'.[37] 'Progress' therefore is what inhibits progress, what turns out in fact to be the very motor of world annihilation. On this point, Wittgenstein comes strikingly close to the view put forward by Adorno and Horkheimer in the opening pages of their *Dialectic of Enlightenment*: 'the fully enlightened earth radiates disaster triumphant'.[38]

III.

We can set Wittgenstein's thoughts on the bomb alongside the work of the German-Jewish philosopher Günther Anders, who was given the epithet '*Atomphilosoph*' (the 'nuclear philosopher'). A contemporary of Herbert Marcuse, Bertolt Brecht, and Hannah Arendt (to whom he was married from 1929 to 1937), Anders devoted much of his work in the 1950s and early 1960s to exploring the relation between technology and catastrophe, especially the threat of nuclear extermination. According to Anders, we have become 'inverted Utopians': 'while ordinary Utopians are unable to actually produce what they are able to visualise, we are unable to visualise what we are actually producing'.[39] This *Promethean gap* – 'our capacity to produce as opposed to our power to imagine' – 'defines the moral situation [facing us] today'.[40] Our society is, Anders argues, a society of machines and technological devices; and it is through these that the great 'dream of omnipotence has at long last come true'.[41] This dream, however, turns out to be the very nightmare from which we cannot awake, precisely because 'we are [now] in a position to inflict *absolute destruction* on each other'.[42] With these new 'apocalyptic powers', we enter what Anders calls 'The Last Age':

On August 6, 1945, the day of Hiroshima, a New Age began: the age in which at any given moment we have the power to transform any given place on our planet, and even our planet itself, into a Hiroshima. On that day we became, at least 'modo negativo', omnipotent; but since, on the other hand, we can be wiped out at any given moment, we also became totally impotent. However long this age may last, even if it should last forever, it is 'The Last Age' . . . Thus the basic moral question of former times must be radically reformulated: instead of asking '*How* should we live?', we now must ask '*Will* we live?'[43]

Surviving the threat of extinction will entail, at least in part, expanding our capacity for fear and anxiety and cultivating a renewed sense of the apocalyptic. As Anders puts it: 'Our imperative: "Expand the capacity of your imagination," means, in concreto: "Increase your capacity of fear." Therefore: don't fear fear, have the courage to be frightened, and to frighten others, too. Frighten thy neighbour as yourself.'[44] We thus need to become *enlightened doomsayers*.[45] Anders distils this doomsaying metaphysics into a short parable which creatively retells the Old Testament story of Noah:

One day, [Noah] clothed himself in sackcloth and covered his head with ashes. Only a man who was mourning [the death of] a beloved child or his wife was allowed to do this. Clothed in the garb of truth, bearer of sorrow, he went back to the city, resolved to turn the curiosity, spitefulness, and superstition of its inhabitants to his advantage. Soon he had gathered around him a small curious crowd, and questions began to be asked. He was asked if someone had died and who the dead person was. Noah replied to them that many had died, and then, to the great amusement of his listeners, said that they themselves were the dead of whom he spoke. When he was asked when this catastrophe had taken place, he replied to them: 'Tomorrow.' Profiting from their attention and confusion, Noah drew himself up to his full height and said these words: 'The day after tomorrow, the flood will be something that has been. And when the flood will have been, everything that is will never have existed. When the flood will have carried off everything that is, everything that will have been, it will be too late to remember, for there will no longer be anyone alive. And so there will no longer be any difference between the dead and those who mourn them. If I have come before you, it is in order to reverse time, to mourn tomorrow's dead today. The day after tomorrow it will be too late.' With this he went back whence he had come, took off the sackcloth [that he wore], cleaned his face of the ashes that covered it, and went to his workshop. That evening a carpenter knocked on his door and said to him: 'Let me help you build an ark, so that it may become false.' Later a roofer joined them, saying: 'It is raining over the mountains, let me help you, so that it may become false.'[46]

According to the philosopher Jean-Pierre Dupuy, what we discover in Anders's Noah is an apocalypticism which signposts a way out of our current impasse when it comes to thinking the planetary catastrophe. For Dupuy, in Anders's parable the catastrophe is both *necessary* – fated to occur – and a *contingent accident* – one that need not happen. The way out of this paradox, based on a new understanding of the relation between future and past, requires us to act *as if* the catastrophe has already happened – or is fated to happen – in order to prevent it from becoming true (a version of the famous 'future anterior' that we find in Lacan). By acting *as if* the catastrophe has already taken place – or will *necessarily* take place – we are able to project ourselves into the post-apocalyptic situation and ask what we could and should have done otherwise. 'Let me help you build an ark, so that it may become false.'[47]

Both philosophically and politically, however, Dupuy's metaphysical 'ruse', which he extracts from Anders, turns out to be a dead end.[48] First, it is not clear why thinking of the catastrophe as inscribed in our future as fate would necessarily mobilize us to act against it, especially if averting the worst turns out to be (as Dupuy suggests) an activity of 'indefinite postponement', an infinite extension of the present. The politics of Dupuy's temporal metaphysics is liberal and survivalist, rather than emancipatory: by asking us to act 'as if' the future is already a ruin, he gives no suggestion of a transformed society to come, merely the hope that we might succeed in preserving *what already is*. Second, to advocate acting 'as if' the catastrophe is our implacable destiny is still to posit catastrophe as an existential dark cloud looming on the horizon. But this is like the case of the obsessional neurotic patient who fears the occurrence of a terrible event in the future (a mental breakdown, perhaps), forgetting that they have entered psychoanalytic treatment precisely because this terrible event has in fact *already occurred*.[49]

We don't need to act 'as if' the catastrophe has happened or will one day happen because – as is now abundantly clear – the future of recurring disasters linked to climate change and ecological destruction has *already arrived*. Our task is thus not to try to avert the worst by prophesying it, but rather to find ourselves *within* the current moment of crisis and catastrophe: to take the threat of extinction as our starting point, and, in this context, to recall Walter Benjamin's words that revolutions aren't necessarily the locomotives of world history, but rather attempts by passengers on capitalism's runaway train 'to activate the emergency break'.[50] The aim, as Benjamin powerfully puts it, is '*to interrupt the course of the world*'.[51]

Looking Extinction in the Face

I.

Capitalism as the time of catastrophe; catastrophe as capitalism's chronic condition: this is the point from which radical thought needs to begin.

In the penultimate section of his magnum opus *Negative Dialectics*, Adorno, not for the first time, turns Hegel's thought politically on its head: 'The world spirit . . . would have to be defined as permanent catastrophe.'[52] For Hegel, world spirit (*Weltgeist*) is the *substance of history*, the spirit of the world as it reveals itself in human consciousness. Its aim is to make itself its own object, to discover its true nature and to become conscious of itself.[53] At each stage of its development, world spirit realizes itself in the forms of life of particular human societies: their political institutions, moral frameworks, cultural models, and systems of knowledge. As Adorno makes clear, however, it is capitalism, ironically and perversely, that has now realized Hegel's *Weltgeist*. To the extent that world history is an expression of the process of this new spirit, it is a history 'leading not from savagery to humanitarianism . . . but from the slingshot to the megaton bomb'.[54] There is no progressivist 'universal history', just an emergency situation in which 'the forms of humanity's own global societal constitution threaten its life'.[55] 'The One and All that keeps rolling to this day – with occasional breathing spells – [is] the absolute of suffering', Adorno writes.[56] We should add here, however, that in our own time – a period of suffocating pandemics, murderous police chokeholds, and megacities on the verge of asphyxiation – even this freedom to draw breath can now no longer be taken for granted.[57]

But Adorno also makes another dialectical move. While the chronic nature of catastrophe means that we cannot assume any progress that would suggest that humanity already exists and is therefore capable of making progress, progress can nevertheless still be thought. Progress 'would be the very establishment of humanity in the first place, whose prospect opens up in the face of its extinction'.[58] It is the threat of extinction then – an end without remainder, 'the most extreme, total calamity' – which makes possible the realization of humanity, the coming into being of what Adorno calls a 'self-conscious global subject'.[59] Paraphrasing lines from Hölderlin's poem 'Patmos', we might say that for Adorno, *out of the danger of human extinction, the saving power also grows.*[60] Another point of connection might be to Freud's 1915 essay 'Thoughts for the Times on War and Death':

War is bound to sweep away our conventional treatment of death. Death will no longer be denied; we are forced to believe in it. People really die; and no longer one by one, but many, often tens of thousands in a single day. [And yet, precisely because of death's proximity,] life has, indeed, become interesting again; it has recovered its full potential.[61]

Looking extinction in the face thus turns out to have important consequences for both Adorno and Freud, although the difference between their respective positions is also clear. For Adorno, the threat of extinction compels us to think about how society as a whole might be rationally reorganized, how 'humanity' itself might (finally) be brought into existence. Freud's much more modernist point, by contrast, is that through the encounter with the real of mass death, life is once again *enlivened*, brought *back to life* – the battlefield of bodies is what makes things 'interesting' again.

II.

The connection between the threat of extinction and the opening up of new subjective and political horizons is given one of its most suggestive explorations in Maurice Blanchot's short essay 'The Apocalypse Is Disappointing'. In the first part of his essay, Blanchot turns to Karl Jaspers's 1958 book *The Atomic Bomb and the Future of Man*. Blanchot reconstructs Jaspers's argument along the following lines. Today humankind has the power to annihilate not only cities and specific populations, but also humanity as a whole. This is a point (as Günther Anders agrees) from which there is no going back; and therefore either humanity will disappear, or it will transform itself. Such a transformation will require nothing less than a 'profound conversion'. But Blanchot also detects something decidedly odd about the style and substance of Jaspers's articulation. Despite the latter's rhetoric of 'change', not to mention the urgency of the issue with which he deals, in his book *nothing has changed*: there is nothing new at the level of language, politics, or indeed philosophical thought.

How, then, to account for this repetition in the face of a new catastrophic horizon? Blanchot provides a clear answer: while Jaspers is preoccupied with the end of humanity, his *real* concern is less the atomic threat and more the extinction of the so-called 'free world' threatened by communism. There is, therefore, no new thinking in Jaspers because reflections on the bomb serve merely as a pretext for returning to old formulas and oppositions: Western 'liberal freedom' as the foundation of all values; death as preferential to 'oppression'. While Jaspers argues that the atomic bomb and what he calls 'explosive totalitarianism' are inextricable ('the two final forms of annihilation'), it is clear that if one *must* choose, then one's 'reason' should be guided by a familiar Cold War logic: better dead than red; better the end of all things than the end of NATO.[62]

What to make then of Blanchot's own reading of the extinction threat? His dialectics of annihilation attempts to open up the new. By putting into question the human species as a whole, the threat of extinction makes visible, for the first time, the *idea of totality*: a global human community. But this totality exists only as a 'negative power'. The humanity that is threatened with disappearance does not yet exist in any meaningful sense, but simply as an abstract idea. Indeed, because humanity has not yet been fully established, it is, strictly speaking, incapable of being destroyed, which is why Blanchot says (somewhat ironically) that extinction (or what he terms 'apocalypse') is 'disappointing'. However, now that there is at least the idea of humanity as a whole, we should work to construct a real 'human community', a true 'totality', one that can, paradoxically, be fully destroyed because it fully exists. Blanchot says, without further elaboration, that this new totality should be called 'communist'.[63]

Blanchot's point, much like Adorno's, is avowedly Hegelian: it is only by looking extinction in the face that humanity comes to glimpse the possibility of its own realization. The prospect of the end places the idea of a new unity on the agenda; it opens up the potential of an awakening to the idea of totality. Or at least that's the theory. But here we might ask if this dialectic still holds true – if indeed it ever did. Does danger signal the possible emergence of a saving power in the way that Adorno and Blanchot both seem to believe?

From our present perspective, the answer to this question must be twofold. First, contra Blanchot, the catastrophe is no longer a future possibility, but (as previously argued) that which, in one respect, has already arrived. This is not (or *not yet*) the nuclear calamity that Blanchot speaks of, but rather the coming together of the planetary ecological crisis, the global epidemiological crisis, and a new period of inter-imperialist war and economic devastation. This catastrophic convergence, far from placing the possibility of a global humanity on the immediate horizon, has instead intensified a series of sad passions and alienating symptoms: surplus rage, hyper-anxiety, cynical resignation, the addiction to numbing forms of enjoyment, identitarian narcissism, collective paranoia, melancholic withdrawal, historical forgetting, the desperate attempt to preserve the 'human' as it already exists under capitalism. What we are talking about here then is a new kind of traumatized psychic reality, a new wounded subjectivity, one that won't be overcome by a dialectics of mortal fear (being scared 'so much that we start fighting for our lives'[64]), but which will instead require a political shift away from the time of endless suffering – a time that Althusser defines simply as barbarism:

27

What is barbarism? Regression while remaining in place, stagnation while remaining in place, of a kind which human history offers examples by the hundreds. Yes, our civilisation can perish in place, not only without rising to a higher stage or sinking to a lower stage that has already existed, but in accumulating all the suffering of a childbirth that will not end, of a stillbirth that is not a delivery.[65]

How, then, in such conditions, might the idea of the whole be placed back on the agenda? Importantly, as Adorno and Blanchot remind us, 'humanity' does not (yet) exist; its existence in the future would require its political construction. We are therefore still living in prehistory (as Marx famously points out), at a stage prior to the actual creation of human society. But it is here precisely – and this is the second point – that we should radically re-politicize the Adorno/Blanchot dialectic. The possibility of a real human community will not simply emerge in the face of negativity (through an encounter with the prospect of our own extinction); instead, it will require the realization that this world – a world of converging crises and political stuckness – can itself be ended; ended through a conscious intervention into existing conditions.

The shift is therefore from the affective encounter to the zone of politics proper; and it hinges upon the recognition that only the collective negation of *this world* ends the prospect of the end of *the world* – understood here not as a sudden death, but rather as an incremental decay, the slow unravelling of intimately entangled forms of life. As Ernst Bloch points out: '*The true genesis is not at the beginning, but at the end*, and it starts to begin only when society and existence become radical.'[66] To terminate the threat of the end (as the biological end of all things) will therefore mean beginning again at the end (of prehistory): abolishing a mode of political and economic life which seeks to tether us all – the *yet to be born* – to a sick but undying present.

2

Extinction Episodes: From the Sublime to the Demonic

A Kantian Earthquake

History, as Wittgenstein reminds us, never quite unfolds in the manner that we expect. Its path, he says, is not a straight line but a curve, constantly changing direction.[1] On the morning of 1 November 1755 – All Saints' Day – a massive earthquake struck the city of Lisbon, reducing it to ruins. Churches collapsed, burying congregations; a quarter of the city's houses were destroyed; a riverfront quay, on which thousands had taken refuge, disappeared beneath the Tagus. According to one eyewitness report, the earthquake 'reduced the whole Metropolis to Ashes; rendering it such a Spectacle of Terror and Amazement, as well as Desolation to its Beholders, as perhaps has not been equalled from the Foundation of the World!'[2] The earthquake, along with the resulting firestorms and tsunami, killed between 30,000 and 40,000 people, approximately one fifth of Lisbon's population.

Aftershocks from the earthquake were felt throughout Europe and North Africa. But these shocks were not just registered in the physical world: they were also felt at the level of philosophical thought. In the first book of his autobiography, *Dichtung und Wahrheit*, Goethe notes that the earthquake, having 'deeply shaken' his own 'tranquillity of mind' as a young child, succeeded in 'spreading enormous terror over a world grown accustomed to peace and quiet'.[3] The disaster 'sufficed to cure Voltaire of the theodicy of Leibniz', Adorno comments in *Negative Dialectics*, without adding anything more specific.[4] In fact Voltaire was among the first to incorporate the Lisbon catastrophe into his philosophical thinking. As is now well known, his 1759 novel *Candide* contains a satirical attack upon the metaphysical optimism of Leibniz's idea that we live in 'the best of all possible worlds'. However, written three years earlier, in the immediate aftermath of the earthquake, Voltaire's *Poème sur le dèsastre de Lisbonne* already takes aim at Alexander Pope's Leibnizian maxim 'Whatever is, is right':

> Oh wretched man, earth-feted to be cursed;
> Abyss of plagues, and miseries the worst!
> Horrors on horrors, griefs on griefs must show,
> That man's the victim of unceasing woe
>
> . . .
>
> Women and children heaped up mountain high,
> Limbs crushed which under ponderous marble lie;
> Wretches unnumbered in the pangs of death,
> Who mangled, torn, and panting for their breath,
> Buried beneath their sinking roofs expire,
> And end their wretched lives in torments dire.
>
> . . .
>
> Mysteries like these can no man penetrate
> Hid from his view remains the book of fate.[5]

Voltaire's poem is a howl of moral and theological despair, written by someone who appears to no longer understand the unpredictable world into which he has been born. For Jean-Jacques Rousseau, by contrast, this kind of agonized metaphysical head-scratching is utterly misplaced. Much of the suffering that occurred at Lisbon was the consequence of 'man', not God – such as the building closely together of 'twenty-thousand houses of six or seven stories'.[6] It is therefore possible, according to Rousseau, to see the earthquake as punishment for a human society that has lost touch with nature.

While Rousseau certainly chalks up a point when he detects in Voltaire's post-Lisbon worldview the moral contradictions of a certain haute-bourgeois pessimism ('you live free in the midst of affluence . . . You however find only evil on earth'), we might nevertheless ask what, philosophically speaking, lies beyond these two responses to the disaster.[7]

In a 1931 radio broadcast for children, Walter Benjamin takes up the topic of the 'remarkable' earthquake. In his twenty-minute talk, Benjamin explores the narrative potential of the catastrophe, informing his young audience not only about the size, scale, and impact of the event, but also about 'the way in which people's imaginations brooded on the strange phenomena of nature that had been observed in the weeks preceding the earthquake'. In the city of Locarno in southern Switzerland, for example, 'some two weeks before the disaster, steam was coming out of the earth; within a couple of hours it had transformed itself into a red mist, which, towards evening, fell as purple rain . . . Eight days before the earthquake, the ground near Cádiz was found to be covered with a vast quantity of worms.'[8] 'No one was more fascinated by these remarkable events', Benjamin tells his listeners, 'than the great German philosopher Kant':

At the time of the earthquake [Kant] was a young man of twenty-four [sic],[9] who had never left his hometown of Königsberg – and who would never do so in the future. But he eagerly collected all the reports of the earthquake that he could find, and the slim book he wrote about it probably represents the beginnings of scientific geography in Germany. And certainly the beginnings of seismology.[10]

Kant's response to the crisis comprises three essays published between 1755 and 1756 in the *Wöchentliche Königsbergische Frag- und Anzeigungs-Nachrichten*.[11] These essays, though still rarely commented upon, mark a vital turning point in the philosopher's thought. In contrast to Voltaire and Rousseau, Kant is clear that the earthquake has no religious significance whatsoever: although devastating and disastrous, it is certainly not divine punishment meted out for 'evil deeds', not an expression of 'God's vengeance'. The only way of understanding the event is as part of a complex picture of natural phenomena. In the essays, Kant offers scientific hypotheses about the causes of earthquakes (the conflagration of a mixture of vitriolic acid, iron particles, and water, compressed in cavities beneath the earth's surface); examines the possible relationship between earthquakes and changing patterns of weather; and proposes various countermeasures to prevent future disasters on the scale of Lisbon ('The inhabitants of Peru live in houses that are built with mortar only up to a low height and the rest consists of reeds. Man must learn to adapt to nature, but he wants nature to adapt to him').[12] Regardless of the scientific validity of some of these theories, what we find here is a radically materialist Kant.

In the concluding part of his second essay, Kant makes two vital observations. First, 'Man is not born to build everlasting dwellings on this stage of vanity', for life surely has a 'far nobler aim'. And second, the earthquake may be only the start of a larger terrestrial 'catastrophe'; indeed, in the 'destruction' of 'those things that seem to us the greatest and most important' what we come to glimpse is 'the transience of the world' – that is to say, *its possible extinction*.[13] Here it is as if Kant has stumbled across something so alien, inexplicable, and strange that he is immediately forced to retreat, to repress the very truth he has just caught sight of – which in this case he does with a homespun piece of moralizing: 'the goods of this world cannot provide any satisfaction for our desire for happiness!' But what gets repressed is of course condemned to return; and this, as we shall see, is precisely what happens: the ghost of Lisbon and the spectre of extinction both stage a dramatic reappearance in Kant's later theory of the sublime.[14]

Truth Is an Old Bone

If Kant's initial response to encountering the real of extinction is to avert his gaze, then we should note that he has good historical reason for doing so. Up until the late eighteenth century, the very idea of extinction remained almost unthinkable. At this time the generally held view was that all the bodies of creation were bound together in a 'great chain of being'. This chain was seen as a single linear series, beginning with God, angels, and man, and descending to animals, plants, and rocks. This deeply held idea brought together the notion of plenitude – the belief that the world is full, complete, and perfect – with the notions of continuity and gradation – the view that all things can be lined up on a vertical scale with no discernible gaps between them. The species comprising the great chain were seen to exist in a mutually dependent relationship: if a single link was broken, the entire edifice would collapse, with disastrous consequences for nature.[15] This state of complex interconnectedness is well captured by the poet and botanist Benjamin Stillingfleet:

each moss,
Each shell, each crawling insect holds a rank
Important to the plan of Him who framed
The scale of beings; holds a rank, which lost,
Would break the chain, and leave behind a gap
Which Nature's self would rue.[16]

While the idea of the great chain of being has still not vanished from history – 'a highly articulated version of it still exists as a contemporary unconscious cultural model', as George Lakoff and Mark Turner point out[17] – in 1796 the French zoologist and palaeontologist Georges Cuvier took a step towards decisively breaking it. Having carried out extensive examinations of what looked like elephant fossils, Cuvier found that the fossils were 'absolutely [not] from the same species' and that 'these [fossil] animals differ from the elephant as much as, or more than, the dog differs from the jackal and hyena'. Cuvier thus arrived at a devastating conclusion: 'All these facts . . . seem to me to prove the existence of a world previous to ours, destroyed by some kind of catastrophe.'[18] It is therefore through what Cuvier describes as 'some half-decomposed bones' that extinction comes to be established as a scientific fact.

According to Cuvier's theory, every organized being forms a whole: a functionally integrated 'animal machine', perfectly adapted to its specific mode of life. It is consequently impossible to imagine any species *gradually* becoming extinct. Rather, extinction must be brought about by a sudden catastrophe: a disruption in ecological homeostasis effectuated by a 'natural' crisis such as a flood or earthquake. As Cuvier writes:

Life . . . has been often disturbed on this earth by terrible events – calamities which, at their commencement, have perhaps moved and overturned to a great depth the entire

outer crust of the globe, but which, since these first
commotions, have uniformly acted at a less depth and less
generally. Numberless living beings have been the victims
of these catastrophes; some have been destroyed by sudden
inundations, others have been laid dry in consequence of
the bottom of the seas being instantaneously elevated.
Their races even have become extinct, and have left no
memorial of them except some small fragments which the
naturalist can scarcely recognise.

Such are the conclusions which necessarily result from
the objects that we meet with at every step of our enquiry,
and which we can always verify by examples drawn from
almost every country. Every part of the globe bears the
impress of these great and terrible events so distinctly, that
they must be visible to all who are qualified to read their
history in the remains which they have left behind.[19]

With this theory of 'catastrophism', Cuvier presents not only
a revolution in scientific understanding but also a kind of
poetics of extinction. Balzac describes him as the 'greatest
poet of [the nineteenth] century'; Goethe credits him as being
one of the leading intellects of the times; and Byron and
Percy Shelley both mine his theories in the course of their
own romantic-literary experimentations. But there is something not only modern but also *proto-modernist* about
Cuvier and his ideas. His invitation that we follow 'in the
infancy of our species, the almost obliterated traces of so
many nations that have become extinct, is taken up nowhere
more clearly than in the opening section of Paul Valéry's
1919 essay 'The Crisis of the Mind':[20]

We later civilisations . . . we too now know that we are
mortal . . . We had long heard tell of whole worlds that

had vanished, of empires sunk without a trace, gone down with all their men and all their machines into the unexplorable depths of the centuries ... And we see now that the abyss of history is deep enough to hold us all. We are aware that a civilisation has the same fragility as a life.[21]

While the catastrophes and disappearances that Cuvier explores are all 'natural' ones (the results of nature's 'intestine wars'), what Valéry examines here is loss of a different kind: the extinction of a certain social and cultural form of life – and the opening up of a new age of 'horror' – as a consequence of imperialist war.

Extinction, the Sublime, and Revolution

I.

In Kant's essays on the Lisbon disaster, extinction figures as the half-thought and the half-said. However, in the 'Analytic of the Sublime' in the *Critique of Judgement* (Kant's third *Critique*) numerous remarkable things occur.[22] First, the tremors of the earthquake can still be felt in Kant's prose. 'In presenting the sublime in nature the mind feels *agitated*', Kant says; and this agitation 'can be compared with a *vibration*, i.e., with a rapid alternation of repulsion from, and attraction to, one and the same object'. The imagination is, moreover, driven towards an 'abyss' in which it 'is afraid to lose itself'.[23] In his second Lisbon essay, Kant speaks of 'the terrible instruments by which disaster is visited on mankind, the shattering of countries, the fury of the sea shaken to its foundations, the fire-spewing mountains', all inviting our 'contemplation'.[24] In the third *Critique*, these same images return, but not simply as 'terrible instances' to contemplate. Rather, they are positioned as integral to the articulation of the theory of the

sublime, which offers nothing less than a wholesale transformation of the subject's relationship to nature:

> Thunderclouds piling up in the sky and moving about
> accompanied by lightning and thunderclaps, volcanoes
> with all their destructive power, hurricanes with all the
> devastation they leave behind, the boundless ocean heaved
> up, the high waterfall of a mighty river, and so on.
> Compared to the might of any of these, our ability to resist
> becomes an insignificant trifle. Yet the sight of them
> becomes all the more attractive the more fearful it is,
> provided we are in a safe place. And we like to call these
> objects sublime because they raise the soul's fortitude
> above its usual middle range and allow us to discover in
> ourselves an ability to resist which is of a quite different
> kind, and which gives us the courage [to believe] that we
> could be a match for nature's seeming omnipotence.[25]

According to Kant, the sublime inheres primarily in nature,
and he distinguishes between two modes of experiencing it:
the *mathematical sublime*, which has to do with magnitude
and quantity; and the *dynamical sublime*, which concerns
power and might. In both cases, the sublime emerges through
a kind of double movement. First, the experience of anxiety
and powerlessness in the face of some vast and overwhelming aspect of nature, something that leads to a breakdown of
the imagination as it attempts to come to grips with what it
encounters. And second, a reversal of this first moment,
which expresses itself as the 'feeling' of the sublime: by experiencing the limits of the imagination and confronting our
own physical powerlessness, we become conscious of ourselves as possessing a pure and self-sufficient reason which
elevates us over nature, both within and without. The

sublime therefore is the experience of ourselves as free and autonomous beings; it is an 'emotion' (an experience in *feeling*), and specifically a 'negative pleasure' (a pleasure that is only possible by means of a displeasure or pain); and, as Kant never tires of repeating, the sublime is to be sought only in *the mind of the judging subject*, not in the object of nature itself – there is, strictly speaking, no sublime 'object'.[26]

The sublime thus operates according to a dialectical logic. On the one hand, it indicates the *proximity* of something (a storm or an earthquake, for example) that threatens to overwhelm and incapacitate us. On the other hand, the feeling of the sublime is precisely what grants us *distance*, provides us with a 'safe place' that allows us to avoid the impending 'danger'. Faced with a void or absence – a point of 'excess' for the imagination – what is called forth is a new strength of feeling, the courage to measure ourselves against the apparent all-powerfulness of nature. In this way, according to Kant, our aesthetic judgment of nature is called sublime not because it arouses fear, but because it gives us the power to 'regard as small the [objects] of our [natural] concerns: property, health, and life, and because of this we regard nature's might ... as yet not having such dominance over us'.[27]

II.

What, then, should we make of Kant's theory of the sublime as it emerges out of the ruins of Lisbon? Is it an attempt to put nature firmly back in its place and to establish the absolute dominance of human reason?[28] If this is the case, then isn't the Kantian sublime a prime example of exactly the kind of 'enlightenment rationalizing' and 'anthropocentric thinking' that has now brought humanity to the brink of extinction?

Such a reading completely misses the radical moment of Kant's theory. Working through the devastation of the earthquake and the possibility of world annihilation that he glimpses in it, Kant imagines a complex, creative relationship between the human subject and the order of nature. The sublime unfolds as a kind of scene or drama, a narrative of sorts. The weaker party – the human imagination – goes up against the power and might of the stronger – nature – only to find itself defeated. But this defeat turns out to be a victory, an awakening in us of the power of critical reason, an awareness of ourselves as *supersensible* beings. This victory-in-defeat, however, far from establishing reason's complete supremacy, 'prepares us', in Kant's words, for correctly 'esteeming' nature. In a final cranking of the dialectical gears, it is only by establishing our autonomy from nature that we succeed in recognizing our *denaturalized* continuity with it.

We might put this point another way: the sublime hints at the possibility of our own extinction. It is something 'monstrous', a 'formless' 'abyss' to which we are inexorably drawn; and it invites us to take a position in relation to it. But it does so in a particular way: through a certain kind of proto-modernist estrangement effect (*Verfremdungseffekt*). In the Kantian tale, we find ourselves seized by 'anxiety', 'horror', and a 'kind of perplexity', which serve to reconfigure our relationship with nature, opening up a new dialectic between the strange and the familiar (something that Freud will later take up in his treatment of the 'uncanny' [*unheimlich*]). According to Ernst Bloch, we find in Kant 'the most paradoxical play of estrangement', and he singles out the following passage from Kant's work: 'Desert, ocean, mountains, even the starry skies, as examples of the Sublime at the farthest remove from human existence, communicate to us a sense of our future freedom.'[29] This passage is wonderfully suggestive. It submits that human freedom – which, for Kant, is the final unconditioned end of creation – is something that the feeling of the sublime can reveal. However, because freedom is grounded on 'pure practical reason' – that is to say, morality – the sublime, as a *brush with extinction*, is also that which directly contributes to the realization of our own moral sense.

III.

We can, at this point, move from practical reason (morality) to radical politics, and it is here that we might begin to turn the tables on Kant, re-situating his encounter with extinction in an unexpected way.

In 'The Contest of Faculties', Kant connects the sublime to the French Revolution via the notion of 'enthusiasm', which he defines as *aesthetically sublime*. Searching for some experience or event that might suggest that humanity has the quality or power of being the *cause* and *author* of its own improvement, Kant turns to the revolution itself:

> The revolution which we have seen taking place in our own times in a nation of gifted people may succeed, or it may fail . . . But I maintain that this revolution has aroused in the hearts and desires of all spectators who are not themselves caught up in it a *sympathy* which borders almost on *enthusiasm* . . . It cannot therefore have been caused by anything other than a moral disposition within the human race.[30]

Kant sees a sign of 'human improvement' in the enthusiastic spectators who behold something intrinsically right in the revolution's attempt to create a new republic. Every people, Kant says, has the right 'to give itself a civil constitution of the kind it sees fit, without interference from other powers'.[31] A morally good constitution – that is, a 'republican' one, which by its very nature is 'disposed to avoid all wars of aggression' – can provide the human race with a 'negative guarantee that it will progressively improve or at least that it will not be disturbed in its progress'.[32]

There is, however, a striking disparity between Kant's admiration for the enthusiasm and passion with which people embrace the *moral cause* of the revolution and his absolute opposition to *revolutionary activity* itself. In *The Metaphysics of Morals*, he writes that 'a people cannot offer any resistance to the head of state [even in cases where there is held to be an 'unbearable abuse of supreme authority'], since a rightful condition is possible only by submission to its general legislative will'. He goes on to describe revolution – and specifically 'the formal execution of the monarch' – as a kind of bad or negative sublime: an event that 'strikes horror' into the 'soul', a 'chasm that irretrievably swallows everything', a 'crime from which the people cannot be absolved', a 'deed' that is 'worse than murder'.[33]

How, then, to understand Kant's anxious opposition to political insurrection? Here we might begin by recalling a remark made by Freud in his 1927 essay on fetishism, when the psychoanalyst draws a link between castration anxiety and the prospect of revolutionary upheaval. According to Freud, the young male child responds with horror when he sees the mother's genitals and discovers that she does not possess a penis. 'No, that cannot be true', the child thinks: 'for if a woman can be castrated, then his own possession of a penis is in danger; and against [this prospect] there rebels the portion of his narcissism which Nature has, as a precaution, attached to this particular organ'. 'In later life', Freud drily adds, 'grown men may perhaps experience a similar panic when the cry goes up that the Throne and Altar are in danger, and similar illogical consequences will ensue.'[34]

Revolutionary activity strikes horror into Kant, we might suggest, because it threatens what he holds most dear: his own philosophical system. For Kant, one becomes morally a 'good' person only through a 'revolution' in one's 'disposition', through a kind of 'rebirth' or 'new creation'.[35] The goal of political enlightenment, by contrast, can only be achieved 'slowly', by a gradualist movement from worse to better. While one should be free 'to make *public use* of one's reason in all matters', this is underwritten by Kant's cynical maxim: '*Argue* as much as you like and about whatever you like, *but obey!*'[36] It is, however, precisely this strict ordering of politics and morals that the sublime negativity of revolutionary action decisively overturns. In the tumult of the First Republic – when politics becomes the scene of violent ruptures, *ex nihilo* beginnings, and spectacular endings – what Kant thus comes to glimpse is nothing other than the possibility of his own philosophical extinction.

Kant therefore recoils from the political sublime; or, more accurately, he attempts to domesticate it. In relation to the French experiment, what matters is not the revolution itself but instead the way in which it allows *enthusiastic spectators* to extract moral and aesthetic capital from it. What Kant thus appears to want is *revolution without Revolution*: an event that can transform the subject – bringing about the aforementioned ethical 'rebirth' – without involving any actual break with the existing order of things. What we encounter here then, in embryonic form, is a version of today's 'progressive' left-liberalism: a politics that is brimming with enthusiasm when it comes to 'looking at' the burning issues of the day – ecological devastation, accelerating inequality, the threat of nuclear war – but which (to adapt Kant's own phrase) has not the slightest intention of actively participating in anything that would change the political and economic conditions from which these problems emerge.

A Perverse Dialectics of Nature

I.

As Kant was finishing work on the third *Critique*, D. A. F. de Sade (the infamous French marquis) was languishing in a cell in the Bastille. Having successfully appealed a death sentence for sodomy and poisoning, Sade remained in indefinite detention due to a *lettre de cachet* obtained by his mother-in-law, Madame de Montreuil. In the period immediately preceding the storming of the Bastille, restive Parisians had begun gathering beneath the fortress's walls. Glimpsing the possibility of an escape, the ever-imaginative writer fashioned a megaphone from a waste funnel found in his cell and shouted to the crowds outside that the guards were about to cut the throats of the prisoners. Sade was immediately apprehended for inciting unrest and moved to the Charenton lunatic asylum several miles outside the city. Just over a week later, on 14 July 1789, the Bastille was stormed.

Nine years later, in 1798, Sade anonymously published his marathon picaresque novel *L'Histoire de Juliette* (*Juliette*). Like his earlier work *La nouvelle Justine*, *Juliette* (whose eponymous character is Justine's older sister) is a labyrinthine tale of unadulterated inhumanity: a defence of crime, cruelty, and unrestrained sexual activity in all its forms. This post-revolutionary horror story is, however, also an Enlightenment tract, concerned with questions of philosophy, theology, and natural science, at the centre of which stands a metaphysics of extinction.

The key section is an extended philosophical 'dissertation' delivered by Pope Pius VI to the lapsed Catholic antiheroine Juliette, where the Pontiff expounds his atheistic view of nature. According to the Pope: (i) Mankind is the result of nature's 'unthinking operations'; and so, at one level, 'man' has no real relationship to nature, nor nature to man. (ii) At another level, however, the two are intimately bound together: if mankind reproduces as a species it takes away from nature the privilege of being able to 'cast new entities';[37] consequently, 'our' multiplication leads 'her' to suspend propagation. (iii) Thus, what most humans regard as 'virtues' (the preservation of living things and the continuation of the species) are 'crimes' from the point of view of nature: 'all the laws we humans have made, whether to encourage population or prevent its destruction, necessarily conflict with all of hers: and every time we act in accordance with our laws, we directly thwart her desires'.[38] (iv) But nature makes clear her displeasure. Through wars, famines, and natural disasters she aims to bring about 'the wholesale annihilation of cast creatures' to give herself 'the chance to recast them anew'. (v) It therefore follows that any figure who participates in this orgy of destruction – anyone who is prepared to help lay waste to the world through 'wicked', 'abominable', and 'barbarous' acts – becomes a spokesperson for nature's desires, the vehicle of her will. (vi) It is the libertine who fully assumes this role: their criminal acts strive towards 'the extinction of all beings', which in turn makes 'room for the new casting nature desires'. In the words of the Pope: 'the criminal who could smite down the three kingdoms [of animal, mineral, and vegetable] all at once by annihilating both them and their capacity to reproduce would be [the one] who serves nature best.'[39]

Here we glimpse the philosophical underpinnings of Sade's empire of *jouissance*: virtue is criminal, and criminality a virtue; propagation is violence against nature, and violence an aid to nature's renewal; the principle of life is none other than death, yet the latter, strictly speaking, does not exist, as there is only the ceaseless motion and recycling of 'matter' according to nature's laws.

In *Dialectic of Enlightenment*, Adorno and Horkheimer read Sade's perverse utopia as the dark shadow of Kant's universe of absolute reason, the negative side of his moral law. The 'enlightened' libertine Juliette, they argue, 'embodies (in psychological terms) neither un-sublimated nor regressive libido, but intellectual pleasure in regression – *amor intellectualis diaboli*, the pleasure of attacking civilization with its own weapons. She favours system and consequence. She is a proficient manipulator of the organ of rational thought.'[40] While this is certainly true, up to a point, it is also clear that what we encounter in Sade is not 'pleasure' as such, but rather that which runs *beyond the pleasure principle*: the death drive, which in this instance involves not only a subjective return to the 'inorganic' but also the total 'extinction of all beings', along with the annihilation of the very life cycles of nature itself.[41] The goal here then is negation in its purest form: a kind of delirious nothingness, an original and timeless chaos.

II.

There are three related points that we can make regarding the Sadean extinction fantasy. First, the desire to completely wipe the slate clean and begin again from zero turns out, in this case, to be a metaphysical farce: destruction is eternally tied to creation; disorder is simply another form of order; death the foundation of new life. Total annihilation, pure negation, attempting to decreate the universe is thus an illusion, as Sade's Pope comes to realize. The other – Mother Nature – still exists: 'When I have exterminated all the creatures that cover the earth, still shall I be far from my mark, since I have merely served Thee, O unkind Mother.' What we encounter here then is a kind of Sadean extinction comedy: the libertine is, as he puts it, unable 'to translate fairly into deeds the appalling desires' which nature has roused in him.[42]

But even if total destruction were possible this would come as a great disappointment to the libertine, as it would be yet another example of his blind obedience to nature's laws.

Second, the kind of radical negativity imagined by Sade's characters is what Lacan refers to as 'the second death'. In his Seminar XVII, however, Lacan makes a crucial point regarding this second death: 'It is just that, as a psychoanalyst, I can see that the second death is prior to the first, and not after, as Sade dreams.'[43] Lacan's point here is that the kind of total negation imagined by Sade libertines doesn't come at the end, but rather at the beginning.[44] What Sade's fictional heroes fail to grasp is that the apocalypse is what must have happened already in order for anything to begin at all. Nature is not, as the Pope seems to think, an ontologically consistent realm that operates according to a set of immanent laws. Rather (as previously argued) nature is perturbed from within itself, and the name of this internal disturbance is the human subject. The problem with Sade's libertine philosophers is thus, we might say, that they fail to grasp nature dialectically: they see it only as substance, and not also as subject, where *subject* stands for the *incompleteness and inconsistency* of substance as such.[45]

Third, shifting from ontology to politics, none of what we find in Sade is a mere relic of eighteenth-century Enlightenment thinking. Indeed, nothing could be clearer than the fact that today's capitalism is moving inexorably in the direction of fulfilling the Sadean dream of an *apocalypse without remainder*. It is precisely this dream that the artist and activist Gustav Metzger detects in the projects of atomic power and biotechnology, in which the quest for absolute mastery and total annihilation can only be realized through a faithful dedication to the perverse:

The opening up of matter and the penetration to its deepest level to overturn the existent unites both forms of research, which are marked by a readiness and ability to enter previously close domains. These domains were not only unobtainable because of an inability to enter them, there were also walls of ethical and religious interdictions blocking the entrance. This forced violation of the most profound taboos sanctioned in humanity led to a conduit towards the forbidden. Atomic power and biotechnology invented a means of destroying all life and found ways to create all life, and placed humanity on a god-like plane. This is a plane against which all religions have warned: the sense of holiness is entirely breached and, in breaching this plane, the human is being shattered, having conducted the ultimate irredeemable sin. This shattered being turns to a golem, who will march inexorably to its destruction, consuming the entire world.[46]

If the moral and religious language here sounds somewhat quaint, we should perhaps remind ourselves of the current stakes. It is now accepted that we are moving towards a new phase of world war: war by algorithm, and specifically the development of Lethal Autonomous Weapons Systems (LAWS) – AI-driven systems that are essentially outside of human control.[47] In November 2019, US Defense Department Joint AI Center director Jack Shanahan (in conversation with Google CEO Eric Schmidt) spoke frankly about a future of algorithmic warfare: 'We are going to be shocked by the speed, the chaos, the bloodiness, and the friction of a future fight in which it will be playing out, maybe in microseconds at times. How do we envision that fight happening? It has to be algorithm against algorithm.'[48] If the very idea of humanity rests, at least in part, on an ability to imagine the other's suffering, then what is being signposted here is a movement towards humanity's end. Today's researchers of destruction, acting in the interests of 'security' and 'freedom', would by comparison give Sade's band of perverse libertines an inferiority complex.

The Paradoxes of Moral Extinction

I.

It is via Sade that we now arrive at a different way of thinking about extinction, one that we will pursue, in its various twists and turns, throughout the rest of this chapter.

In another passage in *Juliette*, the libertine Clairwil (Juliette's bloodthirsty female lover) imagines a crime whose influence would be endless:

> 'I would like', Clairwil [said], 'to find a crime which, even when I had left off doing it, would go on having perpetual effect, in such a way that so long as I lived, at every hour of the day and as I lay sleeping at night, I would be constantly the cause of a particular disorder, and that this disorder might broaden to the point where it brought about a corruption so universal or a disturbance so formal that even after my life was over I would survive in the everlasting continuation of my wickedness.'[49]

Clairwil here expresses a desire for what we might call *moral extinction* – a total liquidation of the ethical. What, we are compelled to ask, would such a crime actually look like? What would it mean to unleash a universal disturbance without end?

Following the attacks of 11 September 2001, the US administration launched the so-called 'war on terror' – an escalation of the long history of US military expansion into a state of permanent war. Like many of the crimes that we encounter in Sade, this event was itself a repetition: in this case of the 1991 Gulf War sanctioned by George Bush Senior. In terms of its disordering impact and perpetual effects, however, the later war on terror (also known as the 'Forever War') was the stuff of Clairwil's fantasies: a war *of* terror, of shock and awe; one involving the extensive use of torture and extra-judicial killing; and one that to this day continues to play out, with migrants risking their lives to flee political chaos, seemingly endless 'civil wars' (Iraq, Syria, Libya), and catastrophic environmental destruction in the war zones themselves.[50]

What Clairwil imagines is, as Juliette puts it, 'moral murder'. But this extinction of the ethical – which goes beyond the act of 'mere' killing – requires a specific form or medium in which to play out. In the case of Sade's libertines, this medium is writing, and specifically the formulas and recipes for extreme sadistic enjoyment that we find scattered throughout the novels. In the context of the war on terror, however, one of the ways in which moral extinction becomes manifest is in the realm of images.

Beginning in 2004, pictures famously emerged from inside the Abu Ghraib prison camp in Iraq showing the torture of prisoners held in US custody. Many of the images, as is well known, depict blood-curdling scenes of sadistic sexual degradation: a guard leading a naked man around on a leash; a pornographic tableau consisting of a pyramid of exposed bodies; and the notorious Hooded Man, made to stand on a box with electrodes attached to his hands and genitals. Clearly these images don't just capture acts of torture: they are themselves active instruments of torture, produced expressly to humiliate or *shame* the persons depicted.[51]

As a specific mode of affect, however, shame is importantly double-edged: on the one hand, it is the most *isolating* of feelings, touching upon that which is most intimate in the subject; on the other hand, it is also an intensely *social* response, one through which the subject is reminded of their relationship to others.[52] And this, precisely, is shame's appalling paradox. As Joan Copjec observes: 'While shame delivers an experience of our interiority . . . at the same time it makes this interiority appear outside us, in the midst of the world. Our interiority is thus exposed as an event in the world; it is revealed as an exposure to others.'[53] What is truly obscene about the torture images, therefore, is their very denial of the obscene: there is no offscreen, nothing that cannot be exposed; and this obscene denial robs the subject of its core. In the realm of pornographic hyper-exposure, the subject is thus forced to bear witness to its own extinction as a subject: a *shameless* power produces the shame of *powerlessness* by recasting interiority as a public spectacle of the flesh.[54]

While these images have now been largely consigned to the trash can of online waste, filed away as so much political 'old news', they in fact persist as the *eternally undead*: spectral entities that continue to speak of a secret tie between past and present. To cite a pertinent remark from Benjamin's *Arcades Project*: 'It's not that what is past casts its light on what is present, or what is present its light on what is past; rather, image is that wherein what has been comes together in a flash with the now to form a constellation.'[55] The 'old' torture images, we might say, only become *fully legible* in the present moment of settler-colonial genocide, deadly disease (with governments happy to 'let the bodies pile high in their thousands'), and ratcheted-up class and racial violence. At the same time, precisely by being brought to legibility, the images also illuminate the inextricable connection between capitalism's exploitation of the human body and its ongoing despoliation of non-human nature — something which itself now threatens the kind of universal and ongoing disturbance that Sade's Clairwil speaks of.

II.

Is moral extinction simply another way of speaking about *radical evil* – something that Adorno attributes to capitalism as a whole?[56] Not if we take the idea of radical evil in the strict Kantian sense. According to Kant, there is a 'natural' human propensity towards 'evil', arising from the 'subjective ground' of *'freedom'*.[57] We freely 'choose', Kant says, whether to adopt or not to adopt evil maxims; we alone are the authors of our moral character. Kant distinguishes between three kinds of evil: (i) *frailty*, weakness of the will (the Greek *akrasia*); (ii) *impurity*, acting on a good maxim, but not out of respect for the moral law (for example, making a charitable donation because it will be tax-deductible); and (iii) *perversity*, intentionally adopting maxims that subordinate the moral law to private interests (hedonism, for example). These three differ in kind, though not in type: all are instances of 'a *radical* innate *evil* in human nature' – the term 'radical' is used here to refer to evil as 'rooted in' humanity itself, not to evil of a particularly 'extreme' kind.[58]

Kant then distinguishes between *radical evil* – evil which deviates from the moral law, while remaining conscious of it – and *diabolical evil* – evil willed purely for its own sake, which elevates opposition to the moral law to the level of a maxim. While the former is a *species concept*, woven into human nature and applicable to 'even the best' human being, the latter is not applicable to human beings at all – not even to the torturers at Abu Ghraib.[59] For Kant, to be a human being *just is* to be one who acknowledges the authority of the moral law. To refuse the good absolutely is therefore incomprehensible.

There is, however, a clear reason for Kant's unwillingness to countenance diabolical evil. Formally speaking, diabolical evil and the highest good turn out to be indistinguishable: both are cases in which the will coincides entirely with the law. Indeed, as Lacan points out in his essay 'Kant avec Sade', it is possible on the famous categorical imperative to will anything (including absolute cruelty) as a universal principle.[60] This quite clearly causes an embarrassing problem for Kant's ethics, even if it is, to some extent, ameliorated by his progressive Formula of Humanity – a formula which appears to strike at the very heart of bourgeois, instrumental reason: 'Act in such a way that you treat humanity, whether in your own person or in the person of another, always at the same time as an end and never simply as a means.'[61]

Turning back, then, to the idea of moral extinction, we might say that while it has clear connections with Kant's disavowed notion of diabolical evil, it will in the end be better grasped in relation to the much more politically interesting idea of the *demonic*.[62]

The demonic (like the diabolical) does not merely disregard the good; instead it seeks to extinguish it completely, without any meaning or purpose.[63] It is a form of life based on pure destruction. In Sartre's words, the demonic proclaims the following: 'I want to be a monster, a hurricane, all that is human is alien to me. I transgress all the laws established by man, I trample every value under foot, nothing of what is can define or limit me . . . I shall be the icy breath which will annihilate all life.'[64] But here it will be necessary to add a crucial twist. The demonic is not simply evil performed for its own sake; rather, it involves a specific deadlock or contradiction: it is evil that is in conflict with itself.

The demonic subject takes delight in subjugating the other, to the extent that the other's subjectivity is ultimately erased.

But precisely on account of this fact, its plan is doomed from the very start. Once the demonic goal is reached, and the other is completely broken down, the latter is no longer able to provide the demonic subject with the recognition that they crave. The paradox of what we might call *demonic enjoyment* therefore becomes clear: in treating the other as an instrument of one's own perverse pleasure – in turning them into a mere thing, reducing them to a kind of zero-state – enjoyment itself necessarily fails; and it fails, quite simply, because there is no longer any substantial other upon which enjoyment might be grounded.

The demonic subject thus encounters the other as a kind of impossible *limit* – as one who is both needed and who needs to be destroyed. It is as if the demonic subject says to the other: 'I am drawn to something in you, more than you. Therefore, I must mutilate you.'[65] The other is imagined to be in possession of something – a secret libidinal treasure (*objet petit a*) – that the demonic subject desires. But in negating the other the latter deprives them of the very object they were taken to possess. The demonic subject is thus left with nothing, and is consequently forced to keep on repeating their diabolical fantasy, to keep on encountering the discontent in enjoyment. But there is a further twist: each blow against the other is a blow against the self. Inflicting bodily pain and calling forth the other's anxiety does not produce a sense of enlivenment, as the demonic subject might wish, but only a kind of psychic deadness. As Kierkegaard's Vigilius Haufniensis perceptively observes, the demonic is a state of 'dreadful emptiness', a 'continuity in nothingness' which 'might be called extinction'.[66] To this we need only add that the demonic can become manifest not only in individual subjects, but also, as we shall see, in the capitalist form of life as such.

Demonic Capitalism

I.

In his 1921 fragment 'Capitalism as Religion', Benjamin describes capitalism as a demonic cult, 'perhaps the most extreme that ever existed'. In the first instance, the demonic figures as a kind of bad infinite: it is surplus-producing activity without cessation – activity that threatens the complete destruction of human existence. As Benjamin writes:

> Capitalism is the celebration of a cult *sans rêve et sans merci* [without dream or mercy]. There are no 'weekdays'. There is no day that is not a feast day, in the terrible sense that all its sacred pomp is unfolded before us; each day demands the utter fealty of its worshippers ... Capitalism is entirely without precedent, in that it is a religion which offers not the reform of existence but its complete destruction.[67]

For Benjamin, however, there is a crucial second sense in which the capitalist cult is demonic: it establishes guilt/debt (*Schuld*) as the organizing principle of social relations.[68] 'Capitalism is probably the first instance of a cult that creates guilt, not atonement', Benjamin says. 'In this respect, this religious system is caught up in the headlong rush of a larger movement. The vast sense of guilt that is unable to find relief seizes on the cult, not to atone for this guilt but to make it universal, to hammer it into the conscious mind.' This production of guilt/debt leads to an 'expansion of despair, until despair becomes a religious state of the world'.[69]

Benjamin's remarks here prove extremely useful for thinking about how the demonic materializes in certain aspects of today's capitalist culture.

In the second episode of the Korean TV drama *Squid Game* (2021), we see the interior of one of the characters' living quarters: a room the size of a cell, containing a single bed and a small desk. On the desk are numerous books, among them, a collection of writings by Nietzsche and two books by Lacan, including a copy of *Seminar XI*. In the latter text, in the context of a discussion of alienation, Lacan presents his audience with a classic example of a forced choice: '*Your money or your life!*' The choice here is, of course, no real choice at all. If I choose to keep hold of my money, I lose both (as the robber will most likely kill me); if I choose life, then I am left with a life without money, which is to say *no life at all*, at least not within the confines of a capitalist society.[70]

Perhaps the creators of the Netflix series were unaware of this particular excursus within Lacan's teaching, but everything in *Squid Game* revolves around a similar impossible choice, one that we might render: '*freedom or riches?*' If the show's economically exploited characters choose to retain their freedom (decline the invitation to play the game and stay in the outside world), then they are likely to remain destitute or to be tortured and killed by the money lenders who pursue them. If they choose riches, then they must renounce their freedom, enter the contest that is Squid Game, and compete in a series of challenges which, while promising liberation from financial bondage, will most probably result in their death by execution. The injunction 'freedom or riches?' thus entails what Lacan calls 'the lethal factor': the subject must sacrifice something, and this something (unless one turns out to be the lucky winner who takes away the game's jackpot) will inevitably be one's own life.

Squid Game then is as an exploration of the debt-despair nexus, and in this respect it presents the viewer with one face of what we might call demonic capitalism. In *On the*

Genealogy of Morality, Nietzsche further highlights the connection between the demonic and debt. He argues that the moral-conceptual world of 'debt', 'conscience', and 'duty' begins 'with a thorough and prolonged bloodletting'; and indeed 'this world has never really quite lost [the] odour of blood and torture'. What the creditor wants from the debtor, Nietzsche observes, is not simply the repayment of debts (in the form of money, land, or possessions), but rather 'a sort of pleasure': 'the pleasure of having the right to exercise power over the powerless without a thought . . . the enjoyment of violating'. Through punishment of the debtor, the creditor thus takes part in 'the *rights of the masters*', whereby he gets to experience 'the elevated feeling of being in a position to despise and maltreat someone as an "inferior"'.[71]

It is precisely this feast of suffering that we find dramatized in *Squid Game*. The 456 contestants, all chronically debt-ridden on the outside, find themselves, once inside, indebted to the masked VIPs who are financing the spectacle by betting extravagantly on the games. These VIPs, each exhibiting their own kind of disinterested malice, want to see blood; they are, so they believe, *owed* a 'good time'. As the show demonstrates (and as Nietzsche and Benjamin both make clear), under the law of capital, there is no liberation from debt: the more one pays, the more there remains still to be paid.[72] In the game, the death of each contestant increases the total sum of the final cash prize; yet this just means that the eventual winner must carry the guilt-burden of all the other deaths, their new-found wealth remaining permanently indebted to a system of suffering, exploitation, and sadistic enjoyment.

While *Squid Game* casts light on the expansion of debt and despair, it does not provide any kind of critique of capitalism.[73] On the contrary, it comes to ally itself with the demonic, multiplying the logic of the very system which it ostensibly calls into question. How, then, to explain this peculiar ideological twist?

To return to Benjamin's words: capitalism is 'the first instance of a cult that creates guilt', and it 'hammer[s] this guilt into the conscious mind'.[74] Indeed, we might say that the only thing one is certain of under capitalism is one's guilt (although its exact origin remains opaque, as is the case for Kafka's Josef K in *The Trial*). But this then creates an issue that Benjamin does not explore; namely, how to deal with accumulated guilt: how can modern societies develop new techniques of guilt-disposal, new forms of purification?

Squid Game offers one possible solution to this problem: it opens up the space for *passive anti-capitalism*. The show performs a certain oppositional politics on behalf of the viewer, reminding them of the 'evils' of capitalism, and this constructed recognition ('Ah yes, this is *really* how things are') allows a certain quantity of guilt (moral anxiety) to be discharged. This, however, has the effect of binding the subject ever more closely to the capitalist cult: for in disposing of surplus guilt via passive anti-capitalism the subject simultaneously succeeds in raising a new sum of *moral capital* that is then free to be spent as he or she continues to participate in the system. Thus, rather than offering a critique of capitalism, *Squid Game* is instead part of the circuit whereby capitalism succeeds in reproducing itself.

The series therefore stages a cynical double move. On the one hand, it *exposes* the demonic, through a dramatization of debt, guilt, and despair; on the other hand, it becomes *part of* the demonic, its 'subversive' exposure of the 'truth' of the system serving precisely to further entrench it. It thus turns out that the viewer's anti-capitalist enjoyment has been in the service of the other's enjoyment – of capital's enjoyment – all along. If there is a lesson to be drawn from this, it is one that must begin by recalling Lacan's infamous 'Impromptu at Vincennes' (1969) where, in an exchange with protesting students, he remarks as follows:

> I am caught up in a movement that deserves to be called progressive, since it is progressive to see the psychoanalytic discourse founded, insofar as the latter completes the circle that could perhaps enable you to locate what it is exactly that you are rebelling against – which doesn't stop that thing from progressing incredibly well . . . You fulfill the role of helots of the regime. The regime is putting you on display. It says: 'Look at them enjoying!'[75]

For Lacan, the protesting students are not aware of the role they play in reproducing capitalism; they do not see that the system thrives off their dissent. But this is not simply to rehearse the tired old view that revolutionary activity always ends up in defeat. Rather, Lacan's provocation aims at something much more radical (and something which remains still relevant for us today): to remind the protestors of the need to further clarify their political desires and to reformulate them in such a way that they resist being transformed into valorized spectacle.

II.

As a system of generalized perversity, demonic capitalism exhibits among its myriad symptoms what we might call, after Kierkegaard's Vigilius Haufniensis, *'anxiety in the face of the good'*.[76] This anxiety manifests in a number of ways: as hostility towards the very things upon which the system depends for its own reproduction (nature and human labour); as a refusal to countenance any immanent limits or to recognize anything 'outside' of itself; and as a belief that any demand for even modest reform (higher wages, reductions in inequality, environmental protections) constitutes an existential threat that must be eliminated by whatever means. As Marx clearly identifies in the first volume of *Capital*, nothing can be allowed to stand in the way of capitalism's accumulation drive: 'Accumulate, accumulate! That is Moses and the prophets!'[77]

If accumulation is the mode of enjoyment specific to capitalist economy, then here enjoyment figures as something paradoxical. While the *goal* of the accumulation drive is given by Marx's general formula for capital – M-C-M' (the purchase [M] of the commodity of labour power [C] is transformed into surplus value [M'] through the exploitation of labour time as surplus labor) – the *aim* of the drive – and the source of *real enjoyment* – is simply the uninterrupted circulation of capital itself. As Marx states:

> Use-values must . . . never be treated as the immediate aim of the capitalist; nor must the profit on any single transaction. His aim is rather the *unceasing movement of profitmaking*. This boundless drive for enrichment, this passionate chase after value, is common to the capitalist and the miser; but while the miser is merely a capitalist gone mad, the capitalist is a rational miser. *The ceaseless augmentation of value, which the miser seeks to attain by saving his money from circulation, is achieved by the more acute capitalist by means of throwing his money again and again into circulation.*[78]

In this respect we can say that for capital, there is nothing beyond the drive's own incessant movement, no enjoyment other than in the activity of endless repetition. Except, of course, that any enjoyment derived from the accumulation dynamic will, by necessity, always be a kind of enjoyment-in-dissatisfaction, as it's never possible for the capitalist to realize *enough* surplus value. Capital progressively destroys the material base upon which it depends, yet it remains disappointed that it can't do so 'efficiently' enough. In the end, what capital thus comes to reveal is an uncanny double-face: it appears as an eternal circuit without beginning or end *and* as an 'animated monster' unable to rein in its drive towards its own extinction.[79] Like a Möbius strip, these two faces turn out to be one and the same.

III.

It is here then, in conclusion, that we might stage a final return to the aforementioned torture images, seeing them now as entirely governed by capital's demonic logic: exploited bodies transformed into spectacle and generating surplus power and surplus enjoyment for those inflicting the harm. But this connection between suffering and profit – pain and gain – runs deeper still.

As the images themselves clearly demonstrate, the business of torture takes place in dark underground spaces, settings in which horror and death announce themselves. Here we are reminded of the pivotal moment in Marx's *Capital* where the author invites the reader to leave behind the sphere of circulation and commodity exchange – where everything takes place on the surface and in full view of everyone – and to follow him into the underworld: 'into the hidden abode of production, on whose threshold there hangs the notice "No admittance except on business"'.[80] What we encounter here, in the place where 'the secret of profit making is laid bare', is quite simply hell on Earth: abused and exploited bodies, illness, hunger, sleep deprivation, scenes that far surpass the 'worst horrors in [Dante's] *Inferno*'.[81] The whole system of profit making, Marx observes, 'mutilates the worker, turning him into a fragment of himself'. It attains its strength, vampire-like, by sucking 'the living blood' out of the human. 'The vampire', as Marx continues, 'will not let go "while there remains a single muscle, sinew or drop of blood to be exploited"'.[82] This is a 'mechanical monster', whose *demonic power* drains the life-energy from the body of every man, woman, and child that falls under its sway.[83]

What we see in the torture images is, therefore, nothing less than an extension of this demonic surplus-producing machine. The violated prisoners share a secret and obscene tie with today's immiserated proletariat, labouring in so many dead-zones around the globe to produce (or provide the raw materials for) the very commodities which, through their consumption – their transformation back into money – allow capital to keep on enjoying. In the photographs, the voiding of the human subject tears open a hole in the fabric of reality; and it is through this hole that we are able to glimpse the entire global system of accumulation which, as Marx writes, 'comes into the world dripping from head to toe, from every pore, with blood and dirt'.[84]

But here it will be necessary to take one further step. The proletariat's being able to *see itself* in those who have been devastated and dehumanized is a precondition for any emancipatory politics today. For Marx, proletarian subjectivity emerges out of a split. On the one hand, the proletariat exists as nothing more than the waste and refuse of society, the excrement of the world: it is, as Marx says, 'the *complete loss* of humanity'.[85] On the other hand, the proletariat is the active agent of political change, the potential motor of world history: the class that announces 'the dissolution of the existing world order'.[86] The two poles are, however, inseparable: only by being reduced to *nothing* – by having to sell one's labour power as a commodity in order to survive – does one emerge as part of a universal class which is the *de facto* extinction of capitalist society.[87]

It is not therefore, as King Lear warns his daughter Cordelia, that 'nothing will come of nothing', but precisely the opposite: something can come *only* from nothing; only less can become more; only humanity at its nadir stands any chance of being redeemed.[88] This dialectic is neatly captured in Sophocles's *Oedipus at Colonus*, when the blind Oedipus, divested of his power and identity, asks his daughter Ismene: 'am I made a man in this hour when I cease to be?'[89] Here we might re-phrase this remark more assertively: it is only now that I recognize myself as nothing – as nothing more than a disposable piece of shit for the system – that my true political subjectivity, my revolutionary agency, materializes for me.

It is, however, this coming-into-being of revolutionary agency that connects us back, in a final dialectical move, to the demonic. Like the demonic, revolutionary activity is itself marked by a terrifying excess: it negates what we understand as 'ethics', 'politics', 'subjectivity', and in this respect it shakes reality to its very core. There really is a sense in which revolutionary upheaval is monstrous, horrifying, and sublime; an encounter with the impossible real. The demonic militant, we might say, carries forward a clear message: do not make any accommodation with things as they are; live as if this world is already dead to you and you are already dead to it; arm yourself with dialectics. The aim here is to create a new political and economic reality beyond exploitation, endless accumulation, and universal fungibility. If demonic capitalism entails the devastation of the earth and the possible annihilation of human life itself, then the revolutionary demonic marks the point at which collective humanity might begin to exist in the first place.

3

The Death Drive at the End of the World

Transience, Mourning, and the Extinct Scene

I.

In his 1915 essay 'On Transience', Freud describes a 'summer walk through a smiling countryside' in which he and two companions – a 'taciturn friend' and a 'young but already famous poet' – discuss the beauty of nature. While the young poet admires the pastoral scene that he encounters, he cannot take any 'joy in it'. For, as Freud explains:

> *He was disturbed by the thought that all this beauty was fated to extinction*, that it would vanish when winter came like all human beauty and all the beauty and splendour that men have created or may create. All that he would otherwise have loved and admired seemed to him to be shorn of its worth by the transience that was its doom.[1]

Freud disputes the view of the pessimistic poet. The transience of things, he argues, in no way diminishes their value; on the contrary, it increases the pleasure that we take in them.[2] The fact that life and beauty (including the beauty of nature) are subject to time, decay, and (eventual) death is precisely the source of their 'worth'.

While all of these considerations appear utterly 'incontestable' to the psychoanalyst, he notices that they make 'no impression' on either of his companions, and he is thus moved to make the following diagnosis:

> What spoilt their enjoyment of beauty must have been a revolt in their minds against mourning. The idea that all this beauty was transient was giving these two sensitive minds a foretaste of mourning over its decease; and, since the mind instinctively recoils from anything that is painful, they felt their enjoyment of beauty interfered with by thoughts of its transience.[3]

The despondency felt by the poet and the friend in the face of natural beauty is therefore, for Freud, a kind of immature response. The young companions refuse to mourn; and this refusal constitutes a rebellion against transience and loss, both of which are constitutive of human reality.

Originally composed as a tribute to Goethe, 'On Transience' was written fifteen months into World War I, while the 'conversation' with the poet and the friend took place in the summer before the war. As it turns out, however, this conversation in all likelihood never actually occurred.[4] The young poet, generally taken to be Rainer Maria Rilke, did indeed meet Freud in 1913, but only in the lobby of a Munich hotel during the Fourth International Psychoanalytical Congress. Among the other attendees was the psychoanalyst and writer Lou Andreas-Salomé (the 'taciturn friend') – Rilke's lover and muse, and a close friend and correspondent of Freud's.[5] 'On Transience' thus turns out to be a work of philosophical fiction – a fantasy about a certain kind of intellectual encounter, produced in the midst of a world catastrophe. According to one commentator, Freud strives in the text to 'work through' his own lost illusions about self and world, performing an act of 'psychic repair'.[6] But what illusions, exactly, has the war deprived Freud of? And where does this process of repair ultimately arrive at? The close of the essay is revealing:

> The war broke out and robbed the world of its beauties. It destroyed not only the beauty of the countryside through which it passed and the works of art which it met with on its path but it also shattered our pride in the achievements of our civilisation, our admiration for many philosophers and artists and our hopes of a final triumph over the differences between nations and races. It tarnished the lofty impartiality of our science, it revealed our instincts in all their nakedness and let loose the evil spirits within us which we thought had been tamed forever by centuries of continuous education by the noblest minds . . . It robbed us of very much that we had loved, and showed us how ephemeral were many things that we had regarded as changeless . . .
>
> Mourning . . . however painful it may be, comes to a spontaneous end. When it has renounced everything that has been lost, then it has consumed itself, and our libido is once more free . . . to replace the lost objects by fresh ones, equally or still more precious. It is to be hoped that the same will be true of the losses caused by this war. When once the mourning is over, it will be found that our high opinion of the riches of civilisation has lost nothing from our discovery of their fragility. We shall build up again all that war has destroyed, and perhaps on firmer ground and more lastingly than before.[7]

Of key theoretical importance here are the essay's final two points. First, that mourning arrives at a spontaneous and definite end, at which point libido is 'free' to be reinvested into new objects. And second, that once the period of war mourning is over, the status quo will (hopefully) be restored, this time on firmer and more lasting ground.[8] There is nothing here then to suggest that mourning might involve a *critical* remembering of what has been; that it might require an *ethical* re-evaluation of the self; or that there might be certain losses (those incurred during a period of catastrophic world devastation, for example) which can only be worked through publicly, by means of a *collective* re-envisioning of society as a whole. In short, there is nothing resembling a *dialectics of mourning* in 'On Transience'.

To take Freud purely on his own terms, however, there would appear to be a glaring conflict between the main philosophical claims of his essay – that transience and loss are essential constituents of human reality, that the fleeting nature of things is internal to their value for us, that the ability to mourn successfully is a precondition for achieving any kind of psychic fulfilment – and what the essay's conclusion actually performs, namely, a rhetorical move against loss, a rush towards restoration, a resolute defence of the permanence of bourgeois 'civilization' and its 'values', albeit a permanence that now has to be achieved through repetition. At this point, it is difficult not to be reminded of Adorno's barbed comment which appears in the first part of *Minima Moralia*, written towards the end of World War II: 'The idea that after this war life will continue "normally" or even that culture might be "rebuilt" – as if the rebuilding of culture were not already its negation – is simply idiotic.'[9]

At the end of 'On Transience', Freud thus appears to demonstrate a painful 'clinging to the object', a characteristic feature of his own description of melancholia. But here we might also make a more dialectical observation. According to Giorgio Agamben, the loss that is mourned in melancholia is itself a *fantasy*, designed to make an unobtainable or non-existent object appear *as if* lost. As Agamben puts it: 'If the libido behaves *as if* a loss has occurred although *nothing* has in fact been lost, this is because the libido stages a simulation where what cannot be lost because it has never been possessed appears as lost, and what could never be possessed because it never perhaps existed may be appropriated insofar as it is lost.'[10] What we therefore encounter in the conclusion of Freud's essay is, we might say, *a spectacle of mourning for a fictional object* – a 'noble' bourgeois 'civilization' – which exists only insofar as it can be treated *as if* it were lost. The political reality of what Freud mourns is, however, quite different, as Rosa Luxemburg makes luminously clear in her 'Junius Pamphlet', written in the same year as 'On Transience':

> Shamed, dishonoured, wading in blood and dripping with filth – thus stands bourgeois society. And so it is. Not as we usually see it, pretty and chaste, playing the roles of peace and righteousness, of order, of philosophy, ethics and culture. It shows itself in its true, naked form – as a roaring beast, as an orgy of anarchy, as a pestilential breath, devastating culture and humanity.[11]

II.

There are two further issues with Freud's treatment of mourning and loss in 'On Transience', both of which cast the relationship between extinction, politics, and ethics in a new and intriguing light.

First, according to Freud, 'as regards the beauty of nature each time it is destroyed by winter it comes again next year, so that in relation to the length of our lives it can in fact be regarded as eternal'.[12] Here the transience of nature, previously said to be the very source of its value, is in effect cancelled out by the *persistence* of nature and its endlessly recurring cycles. Mother nature, Freud appears to be saying, won't let us down, 'she' will go on 'producing'; don't worry about the fleeting nature of things, the true beauty and real value of nature consist in the eternal return of the same. In the face of accelerating climate change and planetary devastation, such a view now appears almost absurd – the relic of a long-since-expired age of ecological naivety.

It is in this respect that Freud's imagined poet-companion turns out to be a much better contemporary guide. Like one of Rilke's own fictional characters, the poet seems to carry death within himself, which gives him a 'singular dignity and a quiet pride'.[13] He refuses the forced enjoyment of nature's beauty, not simply because of the natural transience of things, but, we might suggest, because he also senses *the absolute uniqueness of things* – that they, like us, exist only once and therefore cannot be replaced; and that this, moreover, is something which we have an ethical obligation to register. As Rilke himself puts it in his Ninth Duino Elegy: 'Just once, everything, only for once. Once and no more. And we, too, once. And never again.'[14]

This brings us to the second point. Freud's view of nature's repetitive character, according to which the specificity of any natural object is less important than its place within the great recurring cycle, intersects with a broader psychoanalytic idea in his wartime writings on mourning – namely, that from the point of view of the psyche all objects are interchangeable. Freud is very clear on this point. Libido attaches itself to objects, but if these 'objects are destroyed or if they are lost to us' then libido is once again 'free' to replace the lost objects by attaching itself to 'new' and perhaps even more 'precious' ones.[15] There is something more than a little cold and calculating about this view of mourning, which appears almost entirely focused on restoring a certain economy of the subject. Indeed, it would seem that here Freud's afore-mentioned economic logic comes to assert itself with full force: 'investment', 'withdrawal', the transformation of 'loss' into 'profit'; and at the same time, a conception of the world in which all objects (persons, things, objects of nature) are *inherently substitutable*. From one perspective, at least, it therefore looks like what we encounter in Freud's work on mourning is a certain conceptual merging of psychoanalytic theory and the discourse of capitalist political economy,[16] a coming together of the subject of libido and *Homo economicus* (the autonomous, 'rational', self-interested, economic subject, first suggested by John Stuart Mill).[17]

But this, to use a fitting metaphor, can only be one side of the coin. While the 'economic' is clearly central to Freud's work – one of his three 'metapsychological' hypotheses, along with the 'topographic' (which maps regions of psychic space) and the 'dynamic' (which models repression) – this by no means implies that his work merely reproduces market logic or naturalizes a kind of 'investor psychology'. For one thing, what intrigues Freud is precisely the point at which economic logic gets stuck, falters, fails to operate in the purely rational, self-interested way that one is led to expect. As he remarks:

> But why it is that this detachment of libido from its objects should be such a painful process is a mystery to us [psychoanalysts] and we have not hitherto been able to frame any hypothesis to account for it. We only see that libido clings to its objects and will not renounce those that are lost even when a substitute lies ready to hand. Such then is mourning.[18]

And as Freud says in 'Mourning and Melancholia', the piece-meal way in which mourning is carried out – not to mention the extraordinarily painful nature of the process – means that it is 'not at all easy to explain in terms of economics'.[19]

Importantly, Freud's view of mourning undergoes a significant change. In 1920, his daughter Sophie died in the 'Spanish flu' pandemic;[20] nine years later, in a letter of condolence to Ludwig Binswanger (who had himself just lost a son), Freud recalls his own tragedy and offers up the following reflection:

> We know that the acute sorrow we feel after such a loss will run its course, but also that we will remain inconsolable, and will never find a substitute. No matter what may come to take its place, even should it fill that place completely, it remains something else. And that is how it should be. It is the only way of perpetuating a love that we do not want to abandon.[21]

Here Freud clearly breaks with the notion of finite mourning; the lost love object remains eternally irreplaceable. No longer pivoting on the principle of 'exchange', mourning now appears to involve a consolidation of the relationship with the lost object, an authentic fidelity to that which is absent. At this point, we might say that Freud gestures in the direction of a new ethics. Rather than a resolute being-towards one's own death,[22] life instead calls for a radical openness to the *death of the other*: 'the truly intolerable dimension of human experience' as Lacan remarks in his Seminar VI.[23] Such an ethics will be an ethics of *know-how*: knowing how to respond to the hole in reality that the other's extinction necessarily opens up; knowing how the lost other might, through our own symbolic interventions, come to participate in a specifically human kind of immortality.

Death Drive, Extinction, Entropy

I.

As if Freud can't prevent himself from returning to the scene of extinction, the topic makes a grand metaphysical re-entrance with his theory of the death drive (*Todestrieb*). In his 1920 essay 'Beyond the Pleasure Principle', Freud's 'hypothesis' is that all living matter is essentially pathological, inexorably driven back towards an inanimate state. The essay advances a complex narrative, a fable of sorts – one which marks a decisive turning point not only in Freud's own corpus, but also in the history of psychoanalysis as such.

We can begin by sketching the key points of Freud's narrative.

(i) The course of mental events is regulated by the *pleasure principle*, which aims towards maximizing pleasure – where pleasure is defined as a diminution of psychic excitation and the minimization of unpleasure.[24]

(ii) The pleasure principle, and its aim of keeping the quantity of mental excitation as low and as constant as possible, appears, however, to be contradicted by the tendency of certain individuals to compulsively repeat certain unpleasurable (or traumatic) experiences.

(iii) How, then, to account for this *repetition compulsion* which, as Freud says, when it acts 'in opposition to the pleasure principle' often has 'the appearance of some *demonic force* at work'?[25]

(iv) First, repetition stands in place of *remembering*; and what is repeated is the moment of excitation related to the original trauma. Through repetition the subject aims to bind the unbound surplus excitation that produced the psychic wound, transforming it from a freely flowing state into a quiescent one.

(v) Importantly, however, the trauma that drives repetition is not something that has been consciously lived through; it is not an experience as such. Rather, it is something that lies beyond the limits of possible experience: the trace of a primordial loss, which, in Freud's speculative theory, is the interruption of an original inorganic state.

(vi) A drive (*Trieb*) then, as Freud goes on to say, 'is an urge inherent in organic life to restore an earlier [i.e. inanimate] state of things';[26] it is 'a kind of organic elasticity' that pulls the subject back towards the inorganic state that it once knew. In its clearest form, this hypothesis is stated as follows: *'the aim of all life is death'* because *'inanimate things existed before living ones.'*[27]

(vii) Paradoxically then, in the final analysis, the pleasure principle and the death drive turn out to be operating according to the same logic: while the former serves the purpose of 'reducing tensions', aiming at a zero-level of mental excitation, the latter marks the tendency of all life to return to the zero-point of the inanimate, a state of final repose.

II.

To the extent that the death drive in Freud's theory tends towards the absolute zero-level of inorganicity, it might be read as a metabiological extension of the second law of thermodynamics, the so-called entropy principle.[28]

Having first coined the term entropy in 1865, the physicist Rudolph Clausius formulates the two laws of thermodynamics as follows: (1) 'The energy of the universe is constant';

and (2) 'The entropy of the universe tends to a maximum.'[29] What entropy measures is the level of *disorder* or *randomness* within a given system – that is, how much energy is 'disorganized' or beyond 'use'. According to the Second Law, within any isolated system energy moves inexorably in the direction of increasing entropy.[30]

Commenting on the Second Law in Woody Allen's 1992 film *Husbands and Wives*, the character Sally (Judy Davis) says: 'It's the Second Law of Thermodynamics: Sooner or later everything turns to shit.' This witticism turns out to be surprisingly accurate. When an isolated system reaches a point of 'maximum entropy', this is a state of *thermodynamic equilibrium*. In equilibrium we arrive at the so-called 'heat death' of the universe: a state of affairs in which all usable energy has been expended and the system dies.[31] This state of cosmological exhaustion is brilliantly captured by Byron in the opening lines of his 1816 poem 'Darkness', as if the poet had already grasped the Second Law half a century before its official scientific formulation:

> I had a dream, which was not all a dream.
> The bright sun was extinguish'd, and the stars
> Did wander darkling in the eternal space,
> Rayless, and pathless, and the icy earth
> Swung blind and blackening in the moonless air
> . . .
> The world was void.[32]

The entropy thesis might thus be thought of as the law of a universal death drive; as foretelling both earthly and cosmic extinction. Within all isolated systems there is an irreversible tendency towards exhaustion, degradation, and eventual death. The Second Law's message of ultimate fatality no doubt goes some way towards explaining its enduring appeal for a certain strand of post-war pessimistic thought. In an extraordinary passage that appears towards the end of his 1955 memoir *Tristes tropiques*, the structural anthropologist Claude Lévi-Strauss transforms the entropy thesis into a discourse about the inevitable disintegration of human culture and civilization:

> The world began without man and will end without him . . . But far from . . . being opposed to universal decline, [man] himself appears as perhaps the most effective agent working towards the disintegration of the original order of things and hurrying on powerfully organized matter towards ever greater inertia, an inertia which one day will be final. From the time when he first began to breathe and eat, up to the invention of atomic and thermonuclear devices, by way of the discovery of fire – and except when he has been engaged in self-reproduction – what else has man done except blithely break down billions of structures and reduce them to a state in which they are no longer capable of integration? . . . Thus it is that civilization, taken as a whole, can be described as an extraordinarily complex mechanism, which we might be tempted to see as offering an opportunity of survival for the human world, if its function were not to produce what physicists call entropy, that is inertia.[33]

While Lévi-Strauss's pessimistic *entropology* sees culture itself as necessarily death driven, Norbert Wiener, in his study *Cybernetics: Or Control and Communication in the Animal and the Machine*, formulates a cognitivist version of the same hypothesis, applying the entropy law (somewhat bizarrely) to the human brain:

The human brain is probably too large already to use in an efficient manner all the facilities which seem to be anatomically present . . . We may be facing one of those limitations of nature in which highly specialised organs reach a level of declining efficiency and ultimately lead to the extinction of the species. The human brain may be as far along on its road to this destructive specialisation as the great nose horns of the last of the titanotheres.[34]

At this point, some political and historical framing is in order. Science, like philosophy, is its own time apprehended in thought. For George Caffentzis, reflecting on the history of the relation between energy and labour, 'physics is not only about Nature and applied just to technology, its essential function is to provide models of capitalist work'. More than just a scientific law, then, the entropy principle betrays Victorian capitalism's anxieties about its own extinction: 'The second law announced the apocalypse characteristic of productivity-craving capital: heat death. Each cycle of work increases the unavailability of energy for work.'[35]

It is no surprise therefore that thermodynamics (the study of energy, primarily in regard to heat and work) becomes *the* science after the revolutions of 1848. It is also no surprise that the first formulation of the Second Law emerges directly out of the study of 'inefficient' capitalist machines. Observing the 'waste' of mechanical energy in steam engines, William Thomson (Lord Kelvin) concludes: (i) there is in the material world a universal tendency towards the dissipation of energy; (ii) any restoration of mechanical energy is impossible; and (iii) within a finite period of time the earth will be 'unfit for human habitation', thereby returning to an earlier state of thermal equilibrium.[36] This leap from engine technology to cosmology, from non-perfect machines to a non-mystical apocalypse, introduces into early modernist science a double notion of time: time conceived as the eternally repetitive process of capitalist production and accumulation; and time conceived under the mythic sign of predestination – all life as mere being towards universal death.[37]

Dialectics of the Death Drive

The question facing us now is how to read Freud's notion of the death drive *dialectically* against this background. While the Second Law expresses the irreversible tendency of all closed systems towards exhaustion and death, Freud speaks of the universal endeavour of all living things to return to the quiescence of the inanimate; and in this respect, as Michel Serres points out, Freud clearly 'aligns himself' with the 'findings' of thermodynamics.[38] But here it might be better to say, picking up a line of thought in Althusser, that Freud has to think of his discovery in 'imported concepts'. That is to say, concepts borrowed from the physics of his time, which bear the imprint of the ideological world in which they swim.[39]

To think of the death drive in relation to the entropy principle is, it would seem, to run up against an immediate problem: a blind spot in Freud's own thinking. This is, quite simply, that the death drive cannot help but work against itself, resisting its own goal. If, on the one hand, the death drive aims at achieving a state of equilibrium or quiescence, then, on the other hand, the drives themselves are generators of internal tensions that permanently prevent the psyche from achieving a state of absolute rest.[40] In this respect, the death drive turns out to be a kind of *self-defeating mechanism*, and as such an anti-entropic force.[41]

We can see this very clearly if we return to the so-called compulsion to repeat. According to Freud, the subject is driven to relive particular traumas in order that the psyche might 'master' the experience of overwhelming pain, 'bind' the surplus of excitation, reinstate the 'authority' of the pleasure principle. It is through repetition, on Freud's account, that the subject is able to bring about a reduction of psychic tensions. But the problem with this strategy is that it simply doesn't work. In fact it exacerbates the very disquietude which it aims to remedy. As Adrian Johnston puts it:

> Reliving the nightmares of traumas again and again doesn't end up gradually dissipating . . . the horrible, terrifying maelstrom of negative effects they arouse. Instead, the . . . labours of repetition . . . have the effect of repeatedly re-traumatising the psyche . . . Obviously, this strategy for coping with trauma is a failing one. And yet, the psyche gets stuck stubbornly pursuing it nonetheless.[42]

The subject's compulsion to repeat is thus always a failed attempt at recovery; and it fails, we might say, because the trauma being repeated is itself a repetition of *another trauma*. This other trauma is not the infantile trauma of birth or helplessness, but rather the fundamental negativity (the void or gap) at the core of subjectivity itself.[43]

Here, then, we can arrive at a first conclusion. To speak of the death drive is not to evoke some mysterious force aimed at death and destruction; it is not, as it so often figures in the popular imagination, a thrust towards war, aggression, and ecocide. Rather, the death drive is connected to the compulsion to repeat, to a condition of *stuckness*. But it is repetition – stuckness – of a specific kind: it signals those breaks and interruptions in the 'normal' psychic economy where the pleasure principle fails to assert its dominance; it denotes those points of excess which mark the subject's (human-all-too-human) failure to arrive at a state of inertial equilibrium. In this respect, the death drive can be seen as split: on the one hand, its *goal* is the absolute zero of libidinal-affective quiescence; on the other hand, its *aim* is nothing less than endless repetition, which, far from eliminating excitation, actively produces it. The drive thus repeats the failure to reach its own goal, and yet in so doing it also repeats the enjoyment (*jouissance*) which this negative-repetitive process necessarily generates.

Simply put, then, what is death-like about the death drive is, paradoxically, its *undeadness*: its blind persistence, its inability to ever let up. The drive repeats endlessly, as a kind of acephalous force; and it does so in order to enjoy. As Lacan comments in Seminar XVII, 'what necessitates repetition is jouissance'; *jouissance* is what drives repetition.[44] But here we need to be specific. First, what gets repeated, and what enjoyment sticks to, are signifiers. Repetition is thus fundamentally the repetition – the *insistence* – of speech.

We get a clear example of this in Samuel Beckett's play *Endgame*, in the looped repartee that takes place between the blind master Hamm and his long-suffering domestic servant Clov. At one point in the action, Clov states: 'All life long the same questions, the same answers', to which Hamm responds: 'I love the old questions ... Ah the old questions, the old answers, there's nothing like them!' When Clov later asks, 'What is there to keep me here?', Hamm's reply is simple and direct: 'The dialogue.' What *Endgame* thus dramatizes is (among other things) the impossibility of escaping ourselves as subjects who incessantly enjoy the form of life that is speaking – a form of life, we might add, that appears to grow *more enjoyable* the more absurd and repetitious it becomes. As Stanley Cavell writes (four decades before the arrival of Twitter/X), 'we have to talk, whether we have something to say or not; and the less we want to say and hear the more wilfully we talk and are subjected to talk'.[45]

The second point to make about repetition is that it is never simply a reproduction of the same; instead, it engenders difference. Repetition, as Lacan remarks, 'is turned towards the ludic, which finds its dimension in [the] new', opening onto 'the most radical diversity'.[46] This connection between repetition, creativity, and difference leads us back to Freud: not simply to his famous example of the *fort/da* game, but also to his point that what the subject wants is to die in its own fashion, to navigate its own unique path to death. This desire, we should be clear, is not an impulse to self-annihilation, but rather a desire for singularity: a wish to *die differently*, which is to say, a wish to keep repeating and enjoying one's symptom, in one's own way, right up until the very end. Taken in this sense, the death drive can be understood as entailing a crucial ethical dimension: it is what allows the subject to free itself from the entropy that it otherwise cannot help producing; it is the very *excess of life* which makes it possible for the subject to proclaim (in the words of the old song): 'I did it my way.'[47]

All of this brings us to another point. The death drive, we might say, is split along two temporal axes – a (trans-historical) axis of constancy and a (historical) axis of change. To grasp the death drive as a constant force is simply to recognize that human life will always be in excess of itself; that subjectivity will always be structured around a trau-matic gap in being that cannot be eliminated; that there will always be a tendency among human beings to deviate from established patterns of adaptation and self-preservation and to seek their point of expiration in a singular fashion. Grasping the death drive in terms of change or alteration, however, is to recognize that it becomes visible in different ways at different historical moments. In Freud, for example, it famously makes itself manifest in the traumatic dreams of war neurotics and the *fort/da* game that he observes his young grandchild playing. And indeed, Freud's dialectical move is to see in these specific historical examples a permanent force in which subjects are inextricably caught up.

But here it will be necessary to take a further step. How might we pose the question of the death drive's specific relation to contemporary capitalism? In what ways does the death drive become manifest today, in a new era of converging catastrophes? How does it express itself when the biological foundation on which life rests has been pushed towards the brink, and when the social bond has been deliberately and brutally undermined?

We can turn to two examples, two specific modalities of the contemporary death drive. First, anti-natalism: the view that the human species is morally obligated to bring about its own extinction by refusing to procreate – the ecological variant of this position argues that voluntary human extinction is necessary in order to protect nature. And second, de-extinction, otherwise known as resurrection biology: the attempt to use new genomic technologies to revive extinct species – a move which we will link here to a more generalized effort, on the part of capitalism, to bring about a final abolition of death.

The Sickness of Life: On Anti-natalism

I.

In Margaret Atwood's 1981 novel *Bodily Harm*, the protagonist, Rennie, recalls a piece of graffiti she had once seen written on a toilet wall: '*Life is just another sexually transmitted social disease.*' This sentiment perfectly encapsulates the worldview of the philosopher-detective Rustin

('Rust') Cohle, whose character appears in season one of the HBO drama *True Detective* (2014). In episode one, Cohle (Matthew McConaughey) and his partner Martin ('Marty') Hart (Woody Harrelson) are driving through a desolate Louisiana landscape, trying to solve a horrific murder case, when Cohle is asked by Hart to explain his philosophical beliefs. Cohle's response, almost comic in its tragic seriousness, evokes the ghosts of Schopenhauer and Emil Cioran:

> I think human consciousness is a tragic misstep in human evolution. We became too self-aware; nature created an aspect of nature separate from itself. We are creatures that should not exist by natural law . . . I think the honorable thing for our species to do is deny our programming, stop reproducing, walk hand in hand into extinction, one last midnight, brothers and sisters, opting out of a raw deal.[48]

Cohle is here absolutely anti-natal: humanity should cease procreating and bring about its own extinction. But it is not only that human beings should 'opt out' of the raw deal – we might say, the *ordeal* – that is life, but rather that it would be better for them not to have come into existence in the first place. The world, as Cohle says, is just 'a giant gutter in outer space . . . Think of the hubris it must take to yank a soul out of nonexistence into this meat, to force a life into this thresher.' If one does have the misfortune of being born, then the best that can happen is a swift and early death: 'the trouble with dying later is you've already grown up. The damage is done. It's too late.'

This line of thinking has a rich intellectual history. In *Oedipus at Colonus*, lamenting the hero's tragic fate, Sophocles has the chorus pronounce the famous and frightening lines:

Not to be born is best
by far: the next-best course,
once born, is double-quick
return to source.[49]

This tragic Sophoclean maxim also plays a key role for Nietzsche. In *The Birth of Tragedy*, Nietzsche recounts the story of King Midas, who confronts the wise Silenus, companion of Dionysus, and asks him: what is the best and most desirable thing for humankind? Silenus responds with a 'shrill laugh' before uttering the following words:

Wretched ephemeral race, children of chance and tribulation, why do you force me to tell you the very thing which it would be most profitable for you *not* to hear? The very best thing is utterly beyond your reach: not to have been born, not to be, to be *nothing*. However, the second-best thing for you is to die soon.[50]

The pronouncement of the Sophoclean chorus finds its way into Freud's *Jokes and Their Relation to the Unconscious* (1905), where it is given a particular comic twist:

Never to be born is the best thing for mortal men. 'But', adds the philosophical comment in *Fliegende Blätter*, 'this happens to scarcely one person in a hundred thousand'.[51]

This proto-Beckettian witticism lands nicely – the sombre words of Sophocles are well met by the satirical reply.[52] But Freud himself goes on to spoil the joke. Sounding like an uptight analytical philosopher, he says that the initial proposition, the pronouncement of the chorus, is ultimately 'nonsense'; and this nonsense is precisely what is illuminated by the silly punchline. As Freud explains,

> The addition is attached to the original statement as an indisputably correct limitation, and is thus able to open our eyes to the fact that this solemnly accepted piece of wisdom is itself not much better than a piece of nonsense. *Anyone who is not born is not a mortal man at all, and there is no good and no best for him.*[53]

But here Freud appears to completely miss the point. Of course the never-existent are not in a position to proclaim that 'the best' has happened to them; but this isn't what Sophocles's chorus is getting at. Rather, what their verse conveys is that coming into existence is always bad for those who suffer this fate. Consequently, although we might not be able to say of the never-existent that never existing is 'best' for them, we *can* say – rightly or wrongly – of the existent that existence is bad for them and thus that it would have been better *never to have been born*.[54] Understood in this way, life itself comes to be seen as a kind of tragic accident, a great ontological mistake. As Aaron Schuster neatly formulates it: 'the human being is the sick animal that does not live its life but lives its failure not to be born'.[55]

As we saw in the case of Rust Cohle, the anti-natalist position attempts to provide one answer to the question of what is to be done when life is understood as a disease, as nothing but a futile squandering of organic material. No human life, according to this position, is ever worth the harm; even the most fortunate would be better off had they never existed. In any life, the quantum of pain always exceeds the quantum of pleasure; and therefore the only solution, according to the negative utilitarian logic that anti-natalism applies, is to refrain from bringing any new life into the world.[56] The goal here then is a controlled extinction of the human species. By desisting from procreation we eradicate suffering and eventually arrive at Schopenhauer's vision of a 'crystalline state' or lifeless world.[57] In the words of the philosopher Peter Wessel Zapffe: 'know yourself – be infertile, and let the earth be silent after you'.[58]

Might it be possible to understand this position as a kind of enlightened pessimism? Could we not say that anti-natalism speaks the truth, that in renouncing all optimism about the human species it sees existence as it really is? Our answer here should be a resolute no, although our objection will no doubt sound somewhat counterintuitive. *The problem with anti-natalism is not that its pessimism is too radical, but rather that its pessimism isn't radical enough.*

The first point to make is that anti-natalism's equation of existence with universal suffering looks like a false totalization. While anti-natalism harps on the pains of existence – anxiety, boredom, melancholia, loneliness, chronic disease, bereavement – it has nothing to say about how human misery is unequally distributed along lines of class, race, gender, and geography, or how it might be exacerbated by such trifling matters as the relentless exploitation of labour, crippling inequality, or the continued expansion of a permanent war economy. While anti-natalism is thus relentlessly pessimistic about 'life', it is eerily silent about the profit system which is responsible for specific kinds of life-making. Its ideological starting point is to present reified human relations as the natural state of things: life just is (in Schopenhauer's phrase) 'a business that does not cover its costs'.[59]

But the problems with anti-natalism go further still. In addition to its apolitical pathology, it is also blind to the dialectics of human desire. According to the anti-natalist, the human subject is incapable of attaining any real and lasting pleasure or happiness, and this makes life an ultimately worthless enterprise. But the thing about pleasure and happiness is that they are rarely what they seem. In Beckett's *Endgame*, for example, Hamm (a kind of anti-natalist figure himself) opens with the line: 'Me to play ... Can there be misery loftier than mine?' This is a wonderfully ambiguous pronouncement. On the one hand, Hamm is asking whether it is possible for anyone to suffer as much as him; on the other hand, he is announcing the absolute superiority of his own suffering – a superiority which he clearly enjoys. Proving that the human subject always has an eccentric relationship with its own *jouissance*, Hamm spends most of the play engaged in a discourse of despair ('I'll tell you the combination of the larder if you promise to finish me off') only to find that his unhappiness is precisely the source of his enjoyment. Unhappiness, we might say, always has a hole in it; and it is through this hole that happiness and enjoyment emerge as a kind of libidinal leakage or affective ooze.

This is precisely what anti-natalism cannot grasp, or perhaps does not want to know. It does not see that pessimism is the fixed point around which its own enjoyment circulates. This brings us back to the death drive, to the *excess of life*, what is in life more than life itself. What singularizes the anti-natalist, what provides them with a specific way of going on, just is the view that 'the best is not to be born' and that our ethical purpose now is to bring about the extinction of the species by refusing to procreate. This is a life that sets itself against life, that carries death at its very core; but it is *a life*, nevertheless. If, strictly speaking, the anti-natalist should seek to return to source as quickly as possible, then why, we might ask, do they carry on living? Is it not because the surplus satisfaction found in their own bleak worldview is itself a precious treasure that they wish to protect at all costs?

II.

If the kind of anti-natalism we have just been discussing sees existence as bad primarily for the person who exists, then another type of anti-natalism views human existence as bad for nature. At the beginning of Nina Paley's 2002 short film, *Thank You for Not Breeding*, Les U. Knight, founder of the Voluntary Human Extinction Movement (VHEMT), argues that the recovery of the earth's biosphere depends upon the human species being allowed to die out. In the same film, Reverend Chris Korda, leader of the Church of Euthanasia, says that 'we are treating the earth like a cigar, we are smoking it . . . and at some point there is going to be nothing left but ash'. The Church has one commandment, 'Thou Shall Not Procreate', and it promotes four 'pillars': suicide, abortion, sodomy (defined as any non-reproductive sexual act), and cannibalism (for those who insist on eating meat). The main slogan employed by the Church is *Save the Planet, Kill Yourself*.[60]

This kind of ecological death activism finds its most systematic articulation in Patricia MacCormack's *The Ahuman Manifesto*. According to MacCormack, 'the death of the human is a necessity for all life to flourish'.[61] As the world groans 'under the weight of the parasitic pestilence of human life',[62] human extinction presents itself not only as a logical solution, but also as an ethical one: 'The death of the human species is the most life-affirming event that could liberate the natural world from oppression . . . our death would be an act of affirmative ethics which would far exceed any localised acts of compassion because those acts would be bound by human contracts, social laws and the prevalent status of beings.'[63] Bringing about the end of the 'anthropocentric world' through self-extinction, refusing notions of futurity grounded on the idea of the 'special child', is, for Mac-Cormack, 'a form of secular ecstasy': it 'opens up the void that is a voluminous everything and wants for nothing'.[64]

There is an interesting connection between this dark Spinozian ecological anti-natalism and Lee Edelman's polemical *No Future* thesis. For Edelman, contemporary social relations are organized by the imperatives of 'reproductive futurism', in which the image of the child serves as the 'horizon of every acknowledged politics, the fantasmatic beneficiary of every political intervention'. The child, he argues, 'has come to embody for us the telos of the social order and come to be seen as the one for whom that order is held in perpetual trust'. What would it mean, then, to refuse the child 'as the emblem of futurity's unquestioned value'? How might one say no to 'the fascism of the baby's face'?[65] Edelman suggests an anti-natal, anti-social, future-negating queerness: one involving an unconditional fidelity to *jouissance* and the death drive.[66]

Edelman's ostensibly radical thesis reveals itself, however, to be problematic in at least two respects. First, playing fast and loose with Lacan's ideas, it conceives of the death drive – simply – as *pure negativity*: a negativity that opposes 'every form of social viability' and undoes all ideas of the future. If such a reading is crudely undialectical – blind to the death drive's generative potential – then this theoretical misstep also has political consequences. For if the death drive, embodied in Edelman's figure of the 'sinthomosexual', really does take delight in exclaiming 'fuck off' in the face of the future,[67] then this begins to sound rather strange at a moment when the human species has, in Thom van Dooren's phrase, arrived at 'the edge of extinction'. This situation already produces a new temporal landscape beyond the fantasy of reproductive futurism, one characterized by what van Dooren calls 'a slow unravelling of intimately entangled ways of life that begins long before the death of the last individual and continues to ripple forward long afterward, drawing in living beings in a range of different ways'.[68] No future indeed.

Edelman's articulation of queer negativity bears a curious resemblance to Marx's famous description of capitalism in the 1848 *Manifesto*: 'uninterrupted disturbance of all social conditions . . . All fixed, fast-frozen relations, with their train of ancient and venerable prejudices and opinions, are swept away . . . All that is solid melts into air, all that is holy is profaned.'[69] This leads us directly to the second problem with Edelman's polemic. For him, liberation from futurism consists in voiding 'every notion of the general good'; refusing 'any backdoor hope for dialectical access to meaning'; and relinquishing the cruel optimism that attaches to all political projects. It is here, then, that a further connection to ecological anti-natalism becomes clear. Neither position can think how things might be *beyond* the future as mere replication of the present. Both positions, in their different ways, have absorbed (and been absorbed by) the infamous neoliberal dictum: 'There is no alternative.' Symptoms of the revival of the 'end of history' narrative, and lacking any political proposal beyond pitting a minoritarian vanguard against the mass of normie 'breeders', both philosophies thus offer only a nihilistic negativity: a negativity that ultimately mirrors the auto-destructiveness of capitalism itself.

III.

It might be said that only those who have a future in the first place have the luxury of flirting with the idea of rejecting it. Those reduced to nothing by the profit system are, in fact, highly unlikely to desire the liquidation of the future or indeed the wholesale extinction of the human species – although they may well be up for killing their boss and stealing his car. While queer negativity and ecological anti-natalism both highlight the emptiness of liberal optimism, they nevertheless leave us politically short-changed – locking us into a dull presentism in which the possibility of new collective forms of life remains eternally repressed.

Returning specifically to ecological anti-natalism, what, we might ask, in a final cranking of the philosophical gears, actually grounds the desire for human auto-extinction? What ideas motivate the wish for this particular kind of radical sacrifice?

The first thing to say here is that the ecological anti-natalist appears to be suffering from the specific Western pathology that is *species shame*, linked in this particular case to the hypothesized advent of a new geological epoch wherein the effects of 'human civilization' are said to have completely altered the planet's ecosystems. Thus understood, voluntary human extinction becomes a response to the arrival of the so-called anthropocene: a kind of necessary self-punishment for what is perceived to be exploitative, ecophobic humanity, the destructive anthropos that cannot stop overburdening the fragile planet with its own kind.

But we might also give this reading something of a twist, tilting it back in the direction of the death drive. In his late lectures on metaphysics, Adorno puts forward a new critical theory of death. The crux of his thesis is that because life under capitalism cannot be lived rightly, so it cannot be ended rightly either. The old idea of death as the meaningful conclusion or culmination of a life fully lived is now obsolete. There has been a change 'in the rock strata of experience',

Adorno observes; death 'no longer accords with the life of any individual ... there is no longer an epic or a biblical death; no longer is a person able to die weary, old and sated with life'.[70] Human experience has now become so utterly impoverished that the 'terror of death today is largely the terror of seeing how much the living resemble it'.[71]

Against this background, might we not say that ecological anti-natalism is not simply concerned with 'saving nature', but rather with pursuing a literal attempt to die differently, to die a meaningful death, to *die a right death in a wrong world*? If, as Adorno says, 'the individual today no longer exists and death is thus the annihilation of nothing', might not voluntary human extinction be seen as an attempt to overcome this nothing – to live and to die for some perceived higher purpose, something that is truly singularizing? The paradox here, of course, is that the anti-natalist turns out to be acting just as affirmatively as any other worldly human subject. The affirmation of human self-extinction is just as 'heroic' as any form of tech-utopianism that claims that it, too, can solve all of nature's problems.

Down with Death: On De-extinction and Immortality

I.

In John's gospel (11: 1–44), the story is told of the raising of Lazarus. The sisters of Lazarus – Mary and Martha – inform Jesus that Lazarus is ill; but rather than travelling directly to visit him, Jesus remains in place. When Jesus finally arrives at the village of Bethany, he finds that Lazarus has been buried for four days. Martha says to him: 'If you had been here, Lord, my brother would not have died'; to which Jesus responds: 'I am the resurrection and the life. Those who believe in me will live, even though they die.' When Jesus is taken to Lazarus's tomb, he instructs the onlookers to roll away the stone and he calls to Lazarus to 'come out!' As the gospel then recounts: 'the man who had died came out, his hands and feet bound with linen strips, and his face wrapped with a cloth.'

But what about all of this from the perspective of Lazarus, who clearly does not request his own resurrection? In James Joyce's *Ulysses*, Leopold Bloom puns on John's gospel: 'Come forth, Lazarus! He came fifth and lost his job.'[72] We might also recall the more serious re-working of the Lazarus story in W. B. Yeats's 1920 play *Calvary*. In the drama, Lazarus excoriates Christ for raising him against his will. As Lazarus protests: 'You took my death . . . You dragged me into the light as boys drag out a rabbit when they have dug its hole away.'[73] In death Lazarus had hoped to find solitude and safety, but now he 'cannot find a tomb'. He is thus compelled to die again – to *die better* – by searching for another end 'among the desert places where there is nothing but howling wind and solitary birds'.[74]

This protest against enforced resurrection is given a surreal and secular twist in Joe D'Amato's 1973 gothic horror film *Death Smiles on a Murderer*. Incestuously fixated on his 'one true love', Franz (Luciano Rossi) uses magic and weird science to reanimate his sister Greta (Ewa Aulin), who had died prematurely during childbirth. In overturning death, however, Franz unwittingly sets the stage for its reappearance: unleashing in his sister a passion for the homicidal act. The revived Greta begins by killing her necromancing brother (although this death comes last in the film's narrative sequence); she then seduces the son and daughter-in-law of her former lover, before bringing about their violent demise. Finally, she dispatches her aristocratic paramour – the one who had abandoned her during pregnancy.

We should, however, refrain from seeing Greta's murders as simply acts of 'crazed' female violence. By eliminating Franz, Greta refuses being assigned the position of the object of the brother's enjoyment; she says no to the crushing presence of the *autre jouisseur*, the (br)other who 'gets off'. It is also through the killings that the resurrected Greta comes to identify with her particular symptom – in this case, the need, literally speaking, to look death in the face and dwell with it. Paradoxically, then, it is murder that allows Greta to live by providing her with a singular way of organizing her own *jouissance*. The dead, it would seem, don't always respond with gratitude when it comes to being knocked up out of their graves.

II.

The Dallas-based biotechnology company Colossal has a vision of how to respond to the so-called 'sixth mass extinction' (a situation in which one-half of all species are threatened with disappearance by 2050 as a consequence of climate change and habitat destruction). The solution, they claim, is simple: *de-extinction*. The company aims to use advanced genetic sequencing to resurrect extinct megafauna – specifically, the woolly mammoth and the thylacine (commonly known as the Tasmanian tiger).[75] As Colossal states on its website: 'Combining the science of genetics with the business of discovery, we endeavour to jumpstart nature's ancestral heartbeat ... To make humanity more human ... to reawaken the lost wilds of Earth. So we, and our planet, can breathe easier.'[76]

De-extinction science has been rapidly accelerating over the last decade. In 2012, NYU professor S. Matthew Liao proposed re-engineering humans themselves to produce physically smaller and thus less carbon-intensive offspring.[77] Months later, the first conferences on using de-extinction and synthetic biology were convened by the National Geographic

Society and Wildlife Conservation Society. De-extinction practices range from the relatively low-tech programmes of back-breeding, through to the use of CRISPR (clustered regularly interspersed short palindromic repeats) technologies that aim, quite literally, to raise the dead.[78] Reviving extinct species, according to its advocates, serves two main purposes. First, in the face of ecological crisis, de-extinction takes concrete steps towards reversing biodiversity loss, and in this respect it is consistent with Aldo Leopold's axiom: 'A thing is right when it tends to preserve the integrity, stability, and beauty of the biotic community.'[79] Second, resurrection biology offers a redemptive counternarrative to the pessimism that pervades much ecological discourse. It allows us to move from a 'rhetoric of crisis to a new rhetoric of hope, to create a *promissory wilderness* which includes not only the species alive today but also the multitude of species we thought irretrievably lost'.[80]

It of course makes little sense to resurrect extinct species when the threats responsible for their original disappearance continue to intensify. It is also questionable whether reviving a handful of charismatic creatures will actually enhance biodiversity; as scientists have pointed out, the ecological consequences of reintroducing previously extinct species into the wild remain 'necessarily unknown'.[81] But these criticisms are, in one respect, beside the point. De-extinction is perhaps the most extreme instance of the *anthropocenic sublime*: the attempt to create new forms of 'wonder and awe' on the back of global planetary wreckage.

If ecological anti-natalism invites us to sacrifice ourselves for the sake of nature, then de-extinction asks that we put our faith in accelerationist science to solve all of nature's woes. While these two positions appear to be radically at odds, they are in fact ideologically aligned: both see 'humanity' as the problem, while simultaneously elevating certain humans to an exceptional status. For the anti-natalist, the anthropos is inseparable from destructive egotism; but in advocating for human self-extinction on behalf of *all life on Earth*, the anti-natalist confers upon him- or herself the privileged position of *universal being* – one who can see and act beyond its own species interests. For the de-extinctionist, 'human progress' has come at a terrible ecological cost; and so it falls to a handful of elite individuals – the new scientific masters of the universe – to 'reverse' planetary harm, to 'revive and restore' nature, and to provide 'stewardship' for the entire biosphere.

In the case of de-extinction, the death drive becomes manifest in an even more paradoxical way than it does in the case of anti-natalism. Perhaps the first thing to observe is that there is a curious connection between resurrection biology and the famous *fort/da* game that we encounter in Freud. In the game, the young child (Freud's grandson) repeatedly throws a wooden reel attached to a piece of string into his cot, before pulling it out again.[82] This two-act performance is accompanied by corresponding sounds, which Freud interprets as *'fort'* (gone) and *'da'* (there). Through the repetition, as Freud suggests, the child attempts to compensate himself for the mother's absence by restaging her disappearance and return. But arguably there is something even more fundamental than this going on. As Jonathan Lear suggests, the child responds to the disruption in his world with an act of *courage*, and this courage is manifested specifically in the invention of the game: a game that converts the 'rip in the fabric of experience into an experience of loss', that 'creates the cultural space in which the child can *play with loss*'.[83] Rather than simply a game of mastering absence, then, *fort/da* turns out to be a game of *creativity*: one through which the child develops the capacity to think the very ideas of presence and absence, appearance and disappearance. It is through these kinds of playful mental activities, as Lear suggests, that the child 'enters the space of reasons'.[84]

De-extinction repeats a version of this game, although its version lacks the courage and inventiveness of the one played by the child. It responds to an absence – or rather a perceived series of absences – in nature; but rather than tarrying with loss, it rushes instead to provide a technoscientific 'fix'. This attempt to fill out nature's 'lack', to cork the ecological hole, is quite clearly a drive towards mastery: an attempt to turn everything – including life itself – into a repeatable, replaceable commodity, a source of surplus value. But the consequences of such Promethean moves turn out to be very strange indeed. For if, in the end, there is *no end* to creaturely life but only the possibility of infinite biotechnological reversals and repetitions, then life itself begins to appear under a new aspect: what we might call the *biotechnological uncanny*.

It is here that we encounter a key paradox. Just as the cotton reel in the original *fort/da* game is not, as Lacan reminds us, the mother reduced to a little ball, but rather a small part of the child, so we might say in the de-extinction scenario the resurrected (or genetically modified) creature is an extension of the scientist: their attempt to invent a kind of alternate self or double as an insurance against their own extinction. However, as Freud points out in his essay on the uncanny (*Unheimlich*), the double, originally formed as an 'assurance of immortality', as a denial of the power of death, sooner or later 'reverses its aspect' and returns as a 'harbinger of death'.[85] In the case of de-extinction, the double-as-revived-creature operating as an uncanny sign of death can be clearly grasped. The biotechnological 'creation' cannot but invoke what it tries in vain to cover over: the reality of extinction itself. The artificially revived creature articulates exactly what it hopes to hide: the stagnation and lifelessness of capitalist 'innovation'. The de-extinctionist 'new' is always what has 'already been'; and in this respect it embodies the entire logic of the commodity world, which, as Walter Benjamin neatly defines it, is nothing other than the 'realm of dead things'.[86]

De-extinction – as a manifestation of the death drive as an *excess of life* that seeks to triumph over finitude – thus reveals itself to be fundamentally split. On the one hand, it presents itself as a new ecological theology: the traumatic temporality imposed by climate change is short-circuited by the salvific image of the resurrected creature that promises to 'save' nature. On the other hand, this ecological theology turns out to be apocalyptic through and through. What it reveals is nothing other than biocapitalism's perverse ideological core: all life reduced to mere bundles of manipulable and tradable genetic code; futuristic technological delirium leading, paradoxically, to an infatuation with the past; scientific knowledge in the position of Master, moving, inexorably, in the direction of the disappearance of the human subject. In seeking to 'reverse' death, de-extinction ultimately becomes inseparable from *extermination*: to exterminate literally means to deprive something of its end, to deprive it of its term.[87] Understood in this sense, the de-extinctionist death drive *really does* culminate in destruction; but it is destruction that coincides with the ecstatic enjoyment of 'new scientific creation'.

III.

There is a clear family resemblance between bio-genetic de-extinction and the idea of secular scientific immortality. However, whereas the former seeks to re-engineer eco-systems through species revival, the latter aims to amend the human constitution as such. In the words of the transhumanist philosopher Max More:

> We will no longer tolerate the tyranny of aging and death. Through genetic alterations, cellular manipulations, synthetic organs, and any necessary means, we will endow ourselves with enduring vitality and remove our expiration date. We will each decide for ourselves how long we shall live . . . We will no longer be slaves to our genes.[88]

The immortalist, we might say, suffers from the specific shame of living as a *mere biological organism*, condemned to the human cycles of generation and corruption, growth and decay. For the immortalist, aging and death are not natural processes, but rather evolutionary flaws – defects that need to be 'overcome' by technological and scientific means.

We should note, however, that this line of thinking has its conceptual roots in a set of radical philosophical ideas that first emerged during the late nineteenth and early twentieth centuries. For Nicolai Fedorov, the socialist founder of Russian Cosmism, 'immortal life is the true good, while death is the true evil'.[89] According to Fedorov, the solution to all of humanity's problems consists, first and foremost, in solving the problem of human transience. His project of the 'Common Task' thus aims at creating the scientific, economic, and political conditions for achieving both human immortality and the material resurrection of *all the dead*. We might think of such a project as an attempt to materialize Hegel and to realize Marx. We arrive at a new end of history, an end to finitude, which coincides with a simultaneous erasure and triumphant continuation of the human subject. The negation of the negation, the death of death, is achieved not by Christ or Spirit but through science, technology, and new forms of collective social organization. The class struggle is both completed and transcended in the new universal effort to work against entropy and to recreate the world as an immortal – and thus incorruptible – modernist masterpiece.

Coming after Fedorov – and writing in the immediate aftermath of the October Revolution – the Biocosmist and futurist theoretician Alexander Svyatogor argues that immortality is both the goal and the prerequisite for a future communist society. Death 'diminishes' and 'debases' the individual; it is also responsible for 'social injustice' and 'the antagonism between individuals, nationalities, and classes'.[90] Private property cannot be eliminated as long as each individual still 'owns' a private piece of time. However, as Svyatogor contends, each individual possesses 'an instinct for immortality' which is so 'powerful and unquenchable' that the subject can never 'be reconciled with the order of death'. Death, he continues, 'is so logically senseless, ethically inadmissible, and aesthetically ugly that the question of immortality inevitably emerges in a person's consciousness ... In Biocosmism, every individual – and indeed humankind as a whole – will find complete freedom only in the struggle for individual immortality.'[91]

This attempt to construct a new collective form of life based on the principles of Biocosmism is, quite clearly, a long way from Silicon Valley's current obsession with 'disrupting' death. Whereas the former might be seen as a utopian attempt to think beyond the limits of the capitalist imagination, the latter is an elite project tied to a distinctly neo-feudal imaginary. This ideological gap is perfectly captured in the words of the former Facebook president Sean Parker: 'Because I'm a billionaire, I'm going to have access to better healthcare ... I'm going to be, like, 160 and I'm going to be part of this class of immortal overlords.'[92] In the case of Peter Thiel – the venture capitalist and Paypal co-founder – the pursuit of extreme longevity is taken to sinister new heights. Thiel has long been associated with experiments in 'parabiosis', which include receiving 'rejuvenating' transfusions of blood from the young.[93] Asked about this practice in 2018, Thiel responded: 'I want to publicly tell you I'm not a vampire. On the record, I am not a vampire.'[94] Recalling Freud's famous essay on *Verneinung*, we might be tempted here to disregard the negation and to focus solely on the subject matter of the association.[95]

It would, however, be remiss not to highlight the problems with Biocosmism. And indeed, one particularly compelling critique comes from within Cosmism itself, where appropriately enough it takes the form of fiction. In Alexander Bogdanov's short story 'Immortality Day', 1,000 years have passed since the scientist Fride invented a formula for immortality.[96] Over the course of the millennium, Fride has dedicated himself to intellectual pursuits in the arts and sciences, excelling in every field. Now, however, on the anniversary of his famous discovery he is beset by a 'strange feeling': his enthusiasm for work and life has vanished and he finds himself trapped in a cycle of empty repetitions. At a celebration marking his grandson's return from a long expedition to Mars, Fride announces to the assembled guests that 'eternal life is unbearable torture. Everything in this life is repeated; such is the cruel law of nature . . . Our thoughts, feelings, desires, actions, all get repeated, even the very idea that "everything repeats itself" returns to the mind for the thousandth time. This is intolerable!'[97] Only death, Fride decides, can put an end to his torments, and the scientist thus resolves to commit suicide.

As a method of dying, Fride chooses self-immolation, and specifically the ancient form of burning at the stake. But ending things in this way is not simply about self-destruction.

Rather – and more paradoxically – it aims at *affirming life*. In the story, this affirmation takes two forms. First, aesthetic affirmation: 'To burn at the stake! At the very least it will be beautiful', Fride remarks. And second, an affirmation of the flesh: as the pyre goes up in flames, the scientist experiences a 'terrible pain' and so, at last, through his physical agony, discovers himself as truly alive.

This opens up a crucial point regarding the dialectics of immortality. Fride finds in self-negation a final triumph – a triumph of life. What he comes to realize is that finitude is not what stands in the way of human immortality, but precisely the opposite: finitude is in fact the very precondition of true immortality. The immortalist world that Fride has created is a world of automated existence, empty time, and infinite boredom. It is, as he himself says, a world that is 'cold and indifferent', in which the 'eternally living body [is] joined to an eternally dead spirit'. Only by dying, therefore, can Fride escape this subjective mortification and be reborn *into history*. In typically avant-gardist fashion, the scientist intends his act to shock, to awaken those who witness it. What he wants them to see is that only life that incorporates death is truly living; life that negates death negates itself.

IV.

If it is the case, however, that death must be internalized in order for life to have meaning, then how to square this with Freud's insistence that at bottom no one really believes in his or her own death – which is to say, 'in the unconscious every one of us is convinced of our own immortality'?[98]

In his 1915 essay 'Thoughts for the Times on War and Death', Freud conveys a witty anecdote in which a husband remarks to his wife: 'If one of us two dies, I shall move to Paris.'[99] The point of the joke is of course that the husband, even when faced with only the hypothetical prospect of his own extinction, persists in the unconscious belief that he is immortal and therefore displaces death onto the other (in this case his wife). As Freud argues, our unconscious 'knows nothing that is negative, and no negation; in it contradictories coincide. For that reason it does not know its own death, for to that we can give only negative content. Thus there is nothing instinctual in us which responds to a belief in death.'[100]

And yet, it seems clear that individuals are, at a conscious level, very much aware of their own material finitude, of the possibility that they could lapse from existence at any moment, and that death is the inevitable penalty for all who are born. It would thus seem that we are presented with a kind of psychical antinomy where death is concerned.[101] On the one hand, I am conscious of myself as a mortal subject, whose life has a beginning and an end *in time*. On the other hand, I am a subject of the unconscious, which knows nothing of negation or time, and hence nothing of death as a negation of life by time. I am thus, in a sense, both *finite* and *infinite*: a self-conscious being-towards-death and an 'I' that cannot conceive of itself as not existing. As an actual attitude towards death, this antagonistic deadlock takes the form of disavowal: 'I know very well that I am mortal, but nevertheless . . .'[102] That is (rationally speaking), I know that sooner or later my material existence will expire, but nevertheless (unconsciously) I do not really accept it; I harbour the secret belief that I might be the exception to the rule, the one who turns out, magically, to be immortal.

Thinking about human finitude thus turns out to be a far trickier business than we might have expected. As Kant reminds us in his *Anthropology from a Pragmatic Point of View*: 'The thought *I am not* simply cannot *exist*; because if I am not then I cannot be conscious that I am not.'[103] To this, psychoanalysis adds the point that human finitude has a hole in it, and the name of this hole is the unconscious. But this point can also be given a further linguistic twist. If on the one hand it is only as speaking beings that we come to know death, come to know ourselves as finite human creatures, then on the other hand it is also only as speaking beings that we come to live in *excess of ourselves*, beyond our limits as 'merely human' – subjects of an irrepressible enjoyment that rides roughshod over the pleasure principle and in whose grip we remain forever stuck. Simply put, then, the hole or gap in finitude turns out to be nothing other than the death drive – that residue of immortal, indestructible life that persists in the symbolic, in speech, as its shadowy, pulsating undercurrent.[104]

To Begin Again

In a final move, we might shift the relation between the mortal and the immortal, the finite and the infinite, one step further.

In a 1965 lecture, Adorno speaks of the 'persistence of the idea of immortality', which he connects to a 'paradoxical form of hope'.[105] He goes on to remind his audience of a specific passage in Proust, one describing the death of the writer Bergotte (modelled on Anatole France). According to Adorno, this passage depicts a kind of secular immorality. Bergotte's books, displayed in the lighted bookshop windows on the night before his funeral, seem to promise something transcending finite existence: a persistence of the 'goodness' that Bergotte's life embodied. As Proust writes in a magnificently utopian and speculative section:

> He was dead. Dead for ever? Who can say? . . . All that we can say is that everything is arranged in this life as though

we entered it carrying a burden of obligations contracted in a former life; there is no reason inherent in the conditions of life on this earth that can make us consider ourselves obliged to do good, to be kind and thoughtful, even to be polite, nor for an atheist artist to consider himself obliged to begin over again a score of times a piece of work the admiration aroused by which will matter little to his worm-eaten body . . . All these obligations, which have no sanction in our present life, seem to belong to a different world, a world based on kindness, scrupulousness, self-sacrifice, a world entirely different from this one and which we leave in order to be born on this earth, before perhaps returning there to live once again beneath the sway of those unknown laws . . . to which every profound work of the intellect brings us nearer . . . So that the idea that Bergotte was not dead for ever is by no means improbable.[106]

For Adorno, then, what this passage reveals is that the moral force of the writer holds out the possibility that the order of nature (the order of the finite) is not the ultimate order, that material death will not get the final word. On this point, however, we might also shift our focus, and move from the sphere of ethics and aesthetics directly to the scene of politics.

In an essay on immortality in the modern age, Claude Lefort argues that the great revolutions at the end of the eighteenth century discovered a way of transcending historical time *within* time. The revolutionaries 'passionately set themselves the task of building an eternal city, and identified their own immortality with their political achievement'.[107] Such revolutions moved in two directions at once: they turned towards the past (identifying with the ancients), but only as a precondition for 'opening on to the future'.[108] For

Lefort, immortality thus emerges in the form of a dialogical exchange between that which 'no longer exists' and that which 'does not yet exist'.[109] Or, to put the point more dialectically: the past is made immortal by being re-created in the revolutionary work of the present, while the revolution immortalizes itself by simultaneously preserving, reconfiguring, and transcending the past. There is a striking similarity between this view and Walter Benjamin's view of the revolutionary act. For Benjamin, such an act immortalizes itself by retroactively redeeming (and therefore immortalizing) the past: summoning it back to life, realizing its failed revolutionary potentials, making good on its political promises on behalf of the 'tradition of the oppressed'.

To think this political immortality today will be to connect it to what we have previously called *beginning again at the end*. This can be understood as a new 'end of history' (or rather an end to what Marx calls *prehistory*), in the 'precise sense that the new possibilities for a human society and its environment can no longer be thought of as continuations of the old, nor even as existing in the same historical continuum as them'.[110] Putting the point slightly differently, we might say that beginning again at the end will entail 'a will to create from zero'; which is precisely how, in his ethics seminar, Lacan defines the death drive.[111]

But here we should be clear. This beginning again, which the death drive announces, has *always already begun*. There are, strictly speaking, no blank pages on which the text of history can be written, only those already overwritten with a network of still illegible signifiers, marked by the hands of previous generations. A revolutionary politics of the death drive will thus take as its goal the liberation of these texts *into history*, their coming to legibility: an actualization of a past that has not yet fully existed, a past that still remains ahead of us in time. In this respect, the death drive reconfig-ures political temporality as such. No longer a straight line heading towards some pre-determined 'future', but now, rather, a series of repetitions, or better still revolutions, with each one interrupting the oppressive course of history and producing the new. Such is the foundation of a true politics of immortality today: a beginning again from scratch with one's face turned resolutely towards the unfinished past.

4

Beginning Again at the End

Between Two Deaths

In September 1913, from a sanatorium in the town of Riva, on the northern shores of Lake Garda, Kafka wrote the following lines to his friend Felix Weltsch: 'No, Felix, things will not get better for me. Sometimes I think I am no longer in the world but am drifting around in some limbo.'[1] A few years later, in 1917, Kafka returned to Riva and to the uncomfortable thought expressed to Weltsch, but this time in fiction: in his texts concerning the Hunter Gracchus.

The Hunter Gracchus material comprises two related works of the same name: a short story and a 'fragment', both unpublished during Kafka's own lifetime.[2] The story begins with a cinematic tableau, which introduces us to the quiet melancholy stillness of an Italian piazza:

Two boys were sitting on the harbor wall playing with dice. A man was reading a newspaper on the steps of the monument, resting in the shadow of a hero who was flourishing his sword on high. A girl was filling her bucket at the fountain. A fruitseller was lying beside his wares, gazing at the lake. Through the vacant window and door openings of a cafe one could see two men quiet at the back drinking their wine. The proprietor was sitting at a table in front and dozing.[3]

None of these figures appear to notice the arrival into the harbour of a sailing boat, from which emerges the body of a man carried on a bier. The man is transported to 'a yellowish two-storey house' near the water, where his coming is marked by a flock of doves assembling at the front door. Once there, he is laid out on the first floor and the cloth covering him is thrown back, revealing 'a man with wildly matted hair, who looked somewhat like a hunter. He lay without motion and, it seemed, without breathing, his eyes closed; yet only his trappings indicated that this man was probably dead.'[4]

Appearances do, indeed, prove to be deceptive. For the mayor of Riva, Salvatore, then steps forward and lays his hands on the brow of the recumbent figure, at which point the latter awakens. After some formalities – in which the man's identity is duly confirmed as 'the Hunter Gracchus' – the pair engage in dialogue: '"Are you dead?" [asks the mayor.] "Yes," said the Hunter. "As you see" . . . "But you are alive too" said the [mayor]. "In a certain sense," said the Hunter, "in a certain sense I am alive too."' The Hunter Gracchus is therefore living, but *only in a certain sense*. As he tells the mayor, he fell to his death 'a great many years ago' while hunting a chamois in the Black Forest, and yet he remains alive because his 'death ship lost its way'. What caused this to happen is not exactly clear. Maybe 'a wrong turn of the wheel' or 'a moment's absence of mind' on the part of the ship's captain, Gracchus suggests. What is clear, however, is that the Hunter has *missed his encounter with death* and is thus condemned to 'remain on earth', his vessel blown about by the winds on the 'earthly waters'.[5]

Whereas Kafka's canonical mid-period works ('The Judgement', *The Metamorphosis*, 'In the Penal Colony', and *The Trial*) all culminate in death scenes, the protagonists of the 1917 short stories ('The Country Doctor', 'The Cares of a

Family Man', 'The Bucket Rider', and 'The Hunter Grac-chus') are all marked by the fact that they are unable to die.[6] In one of his reflections on the Gracchus tale, Adorno sug-gests that the Hunter is the bourgeois class that has itself 'failed to die'.[7] While such a reading makes good on Ador-no's claim that politics lodges itself most deeply in modernist works that present themselves as politically dead, here we might push this point even further, shifting it more concretely in the direction of our current conjuncture.[8]

The Hunter Gracchus is *undead*: while he is 'always in motion', he nevertheless goes on without a foreseeable end and therefore without a purpose.[9] He exists in a twilight world, an uncanny third space between the living and the dead. His survival figures as a kind of existential insomnia from which there is no clear line of escape. Putting the point in more explicitly psychoanalytic terms, we might say that Gracchus occupies a zone *between two deaths*. Lacan famously discusses this extraterritorial domain in relation to Sophocles's heroine Antigone.[10] On account of the latter's refusal to compromise on her desire to secure a burial for her brother Polynices – against the orders of Creon (her uncle and king of Thebes) – Antigone is symbolically mur-dered: buried alive in a tomb, cancelled from the world of the living (although she is not yet physically dead). As she laments:

> No wedding-day; no marriage music;
> Death will be all my bridal dower.
> . . .
> No friend to weep at my banishment
> To a rock-hewn chamber of endless durance
> In a strange cold tomb alone to linger
> Lost between life and death forever.[11]

While Gracchus and Antigone both find themselves forced to live their own deaths, their cases are nevertheless reversed in two distinct ways. First, Gracchus's status as undead derives from the fact that his symbolic death has been interrupted (his 'death ship', he claims, has veered off course). Antigone, by contrast, is symbolically dead (*persona non grata*, excluded from the social body) but biologically she lives on (at least until her eventual suicide). Second, Antigone knows full well that she has transgressed the law, and indeed she provides a wonderfully eccentric explanation for her act of defiance: 'I could have had another husband, and by him other sons, if one were lost; but, father and mother lost, where would I get another brother?'[12] Gracchus, on the other hand, cannot understand or explain his situation beyond endlessly repeating the tale of his accident. When asked by the mayor if he might bear some responsibility for his 'terrible fate', he abruptly replies: 'None.'[13] The mayor then asks, 'but then whose is the guilt?', to which Gracchus responds: 'the boatman's'. But the boatman cannot be responsible for Gracchus's predicament if the latter's ship 'has no rudder' and is driven only 'by the wind that blows in the undermost regions of death'.[14]

Cracks in the Hunter's narrative begin to appear. Who – or what – has really prevented the man from the Black Forest from dying, condemning him to a state of eternal wandering? Gracchus's final speeches to the mayor provide an important clue:

I am forever on the great stair that leads up to [the next world]. On that infinitely wide and spacious stair I clamber about, sometimes up, sometimes down, sometimes on the right, sometimes on the left, always in motion . . . But when I make a supreme flight and see the gate actually shining before me I awaken presently on my old ship, still stranded forlornly in some earthly sea or other. The fundamental error of my onetime death grins at me as I lie in my cabin . . .

Nobody will read what I say here, no one will come to help me; even if all the people were commanded to help me, every door and window would remain shut, everybody would take to bed and draw the bedclothes over his head, the whole earth would become an inn for the night . . . The thought of helping me is an illness that has to be cured by taking to one's bed.[15]

Here, then, we might suggest the following reading. *If anyone is responsible for Gracchus's undeadness it is Gracchus himself.* He cannot die because he cannot stop lamenting the fact that he is not dead, cannot stop turning over – and therefore secretly enjoying – the agonies of his own situation. Fantasies of a self beyond help, endlessly recycled tales of wounded innocence, nostalgic reflections about the good old days when his 'labours were blessed': Gracchus is locked into a discourse of despair and it is precisely this that holds him in limbo. To cite a wonderfully pertinent passage from Kierkegaard's *The Sickness unto Death*: 'The torment of despair is precisely [the] inability to die . . . To be sick unto death is to be unable to die, yet not as if there were hope of life; no, the hopelessness is that there is not even the ultimate hope [of] death . . . Despair is the hopelessness of not even being able to die.'[16] For Gracchus, then, there is no death and no life, no departure and no arrival, no damnation and no salvation; just a restless wandering around in perpetual torment, compulsively repeating his 'old, old story'.[17]

And yet, this isn't all. For if despair proves to be key to Gracchus's predicament, then we also need to grasp despair as something dialectical. As Kierkegaard's pseudonym Anti-Climacus paradoxically suggests: despair is the most dangerous illness which, at the same time, is the worst misfortune never to have suffered from.[18] It is both a curse and a blessing; something to be both regretted and affirmed. Consumed by despair, the subject is not itself, but it becomes itself only by having despaired. The way out of despair, then, is through despair itself: one must 'despair with a vengeance, despair to the full, so that the life of the spirit can break through from the ground up'.[19] Or as Anti-Climacus puts it elsewhere: to arrive at the truth 'one must go through every negativity, for the old legend about breaking a certain magic spell is true: the piece has to be played through backwards or the spell is not broken'.[20]

Looked at from this perspective, the problem with Gracchus's despair is, quite simply, that it *isn't radical enough* – it doesn't go *right to the very end*. He still longs to 'solve' the riddle of his accident; still wants reassurance from the big Other (Mayor Salvatore) that he hasn't 'sinned'; still secretly hopes that the townspeople might eventually rise from their beds and 'come to help' him. Except, of course, that all this is just part of his problem. Only resolute negativity – the courage of militant resignation – would allow the Hunter to finally bring his living death to a definitive end.

We can cast this dialectics of despair in more directly political terms. Despair, we might say, is born out of social disrepair, a disintegration of the social bond. If despair is, in one respect, capitalism's 'final ideology', then it also implies a total divestment of hope from the system that produces it, a rejection of its endless false promises.[21] Conceived of dialectically, despair is not the belief that nothing would be better than something; rather, it is a revolt against *what merely is* – a desire (however concealed or inchoate) that things should be otherwise. In this respect, despair is a negative passion that can also function (in Fredric Jameson's phrase) as a 'class passion', a revolutionary affect.[22] By abstaining from the 'positive', by opening ourselves up to the force of despair, we arrive (potentially at least) at a properly political truth: the problems we confront cannot be resolved within the existing framework, and so it is the framework itself that must be transformed.

We thus despair so that despair won't be given the final word, so that at some future point we can – collectively – have done with the despairing mode of life altogether. Indeed, despair already points in the direction of its own overcoming. As Adorno observes in *Negative Dialectics*: 'Grayness could not fill us with despair, if our minds didn't harbour the concept of different colours, scattered traces of which are not absent from the negative whole. The traces always come from the past, and our hopes come from their counterpart, from that which was or is doomed.'[23]

Thus understood, Kafka's famous remark that 'there is hope, an infinite amount of hope, just not for us', can be given a new twist. We might instead say that hope can only be arrived at by way of despair; but even then it is only ever hope for the hopeless, the dead – those whose past dreams of liberation it remains our political duty to summon back to life in the here and now.[24]

Time and *Melancholia*

I.

Gracchus's predicament – suspended between two deaths, caught in a seemingly interminable crisis – provides us with a starting point for rethinking the temporality of the present.

According to the critic Frank Kermode, our preoccupation with endings derives 'from a common desire to defeat chronicity, the intolerable idea that we live within an order of events between which there is no relation, pattern, mutuality, or intelligible progression'.[25] This defence against chronicity can be found in fictional narratives, in apocalyptic religious texts (like the Books of Daniel and Revelation), and even in the way we hear the sound of a ticking clock:

> In referring to the sound of a clock not as 'tick-tick' but as 'tick-tock' we substitute a fiction for an actual acoustic event, distinguishing between the *genesis* of 'tick' and *apocalypse* of 'tock', and conferring on the interval between them a significance it would otherwise lack. The ... end purges the simple chronicity. It achieves a 'temporal integration' – it converts a blank into a *kairos*, charges it with meaning.[26]

For Kermode, we thus give shape to time by transforming the merely successive 'tick-tick-tick' into the 'tick-tock' of a meaningful 'plot'. However, because the 'tick' – the *beginning* – has in one sense always already taken place, it is the 'tock' – the *ending* or *sense of an ending* – which ultimately bestows meaning on the temporal structure as a whole.

But what to make of this in our own period, when the 'plot' appears to have been well and truly lost? Perhaps the first thing to say is that it is no longer clear that endings invest time with significant shape and meaning, at least not in the way that Kermode suggests. We live in an epoch of monumental endings (and possible worse endings to come), in which the very foundations of life quake beneath our feet – climate and ecological catastrophe, the threat of nuclear war, accelerating economic and social turmoil. And yet, rather than saving us from mere chronicity (the interminable 'tick-tick-tick'), such endings seem to consign us to it all the more. We thus appear to have entered what Eric Cazdyn describes as 'a new chronic mode': 'a meantime with no end . . . an undying present that remains forever sick'.[27]

It goes without saying that time is not experienced in a uniform way. Capitalism has uneven effects across different bodies and spaces, and this produces different temporalities, which undergird different subjective economies of attention, affect, and enjoyment. We break, bend, and perish at different speeds, subject to different external and internal forces, which themselves acquire their own rhythm. But there is a basic Marxist principle that needs to be retained and taken as a starting point here. Namely, that 'temporality as an existential phenomenon . . . is something generated by the mode of production itself'.[28] This does not mean that there is a temporality of capitalism as such, but rather that the complex and multi-layered temporality of any conjuncture will be determined by where exactly the system is at, at a given historical moment. This connection between time and economy is neatly captured by Fredric Jameson in an essay from the early 2000s:

> The dynamics of the stock market need to be disentangled from the older cyclical rhythms of capitalism . . . The futures of the stock market . . . come to be deeply intertwined with the way we live . . . By the same token, the new rhythms are transmitted to cultural production in the form of the narratives we consume and the stories we tell ourselves, about our history fully as much as about our individual experience . . . Th[e] situation [can be] characterized [in terms of] a dramatic and alarming shrinkage of existential time and the reduction to a present that hardly qualifies as such any longer, given the virtual effacement of

that past and future that can alone define a present in the first place.[29]

There is an uncanny quality about this passage. While it accurately grasps the contemporary moment, it seems, at the same time, strangely out of date. For it so clearly arrives before the global financial crisis of 2007–9 and the long depression that followed; before the mass human extinction event of Covid-19 and the temporal suspension of lockdowns; and before the arrival of the current age of digital nihilism in which environmental, economic, and geo-political crises are themselves integrated into a chaotic and seemingly never-ending world of scrolling, browsing, clicks, and likes.

In this context, temporal logics begin to shift, subtly but significantly. The past, far from having been simply erased, comes instead to flood the present: electronic and algorithmic systems of memory engulf the subject, producing not just waves of nostalgia but, more troublingly, a present that is now, in one sense, located in the mythologized near past. The future, likewise, is not merely cancelled; rather, it appears to draw ever nearer like some terrifying and uncontrollable force, threatening scenarios that cannot even be calculated. But this menacing future is itself curious in two respects. First, it seems that it can only be grasped, temporally and experientially, via a set of stock dystopian fantasies (from Cormac McCarthy's *The Road* to Roland Emmerich's *The Day after Tomorrow*), which are themselves the waste products of a stagnant culture industry. And second, the catastrophe that is anxiously awaited has, in one respect, already happened, meaning that we find ourselves anticipating what is in fact unfolding. Contemporary catastrophe, we might say, thus appears precisely in the guise of the *still-to-come*.

Temporally speaking, then, we appear to find ourselves stuck in an arrested time: unable to move either fully forwards (into a qualitatively different future) or fully backwards (into the significant historical past). Caught within a crisis that is not a period of transition but instead a protracted state of disruption and stagnation, time loses its flow and the expanding present acquires the character of a limbo state.[30]

What can be done in such a situation? Is it possible to think rupture in the context of a stuck and omnipresent present? Or, more dialectically stated, can rupture – and thus a renewed sense of past, present, and future – be conjured out of stuckness itself?[31] This is, of course, a different way of asking again one of the central questions of the book: namely, can a politics proper – and thus an alternate temporality – be rediscovered *at the end*?

II.

Lars von Trier's *Melancholia* (2011) begins (following its prologue) with a scene in which a newly married couple – Justine (Kirsten Dunst) and Michael (Alexander Skarsgård) – find themselves literally stuck: their stretch limousine is far too large for the narrow, winding country pathway it is attempting to navigate. The vehicle edges forward a few feet, stops, reverses, then stops again: it can't go on, won't go on; the scene seems interminable; the limo, we might say, is trapped in limbo. At one point Michael takes over from the chauffeur and tries to accomplish the drive, with Justine as a backseat navigator. 'You aren't even looking', he complains. To which his new wife ominously replies: 'Well, I can see it's not looking good.'

The destination they are heading for is their own wedding reception, an occasion held at a grand estate owned by Justine's wealthy brother-in-law John (Kiefer Sutherland) and her sister Claire (Charlotte Gainsbourg). When the couple eventually arrive on foot it is already dark, and the house exudes its own strange atemporality: generically 'magnificent', isolated, and self-contained, surrounded by perfectly manicured lawns, large forests, and a golf course. The newlyweds are duly reprimanded by Claire for their late arrival, which has disrupted the day's strict timetable. Meanwhile John reminds them that he has paid for 'the most expensive wedding planner on the planet'. The hosts are acutely anxious, much more so than the bride and groom. For the former couple, it is as if any minor interruption of bourgeois order, routine, and scheduling could itself herald the end of the world.

The film will not, however, be a typical family melodrama, as the prologue already makes clear. This eight-minute lyrical sequence presents us with a haunting visual tableau in which the major concerns of the film are announced: Justine's desolate face staring blankly into the camera, behind which dead birds fall softly from the sky; Bruegel's painting *The Hunters in the Snow* (1565), which slowly catches fire; Claire desperately clinging to her young son, Leo (Cameron Spurr), as her feet sink into the liquifying ground; Hubble-style footage of the earth and a planet we will later come to know as Melancholia; Justine trudging through the forest in her bridal gown, straining against tendrils of thick woolly yarn wrapped around her wrists and ankles; and finally Melancholia colliding with the earth in an apocalyptic embrace. Behind the images, the prelude to Wagner's opera *Tristan and Isolde* plays on. Taken together, the visuals (presented in extreme slow motion) and the score (the unresolved dissonance of the famous Tristan chord) produce a sense of eternally suspended time. Extinction thus comes to figure here less as a literal end of all things and more as a temporal and affective state: a state of exhaustion; of hanging in-between; of never quite dying, but being already dead.

Melancholia is, we might say, a film *about* time – and indeed the politics of time; but it is also a capitalist fable of sorts, one that allows us to re-think the question of what it might mean to begin again at the end.

Following the prologue, the film is divided into two chapters: 'Part One: Justine' and 'Part Two: Claire'. In the first part, the narrative centres on the evening of Justine's wedding: point-less bourgeois rituals, inappropriate and self-serving speeches, tiresome musical entertainment – all overseen by Claire's obsessive timekeeping. But things do not go according to plan. Justine, caught in a thick fog of depression, keeps disap-pearing, straying beyond the boundaries of prescribed time.[32] First, she leaves the house during the festivities and drives a golf cart to the eighteenth green, where she squats down and urinates. Later, at the moment when the guests are waiting for the bride and groom to cut the cake, Justine decides to retreat upstairs and take a bath. Finally, when Michael attempts to consummate the marriage she pushes him away in disgust, pursuing instead a random sexual encounter with the nephew of her obnoxious boss. On one reading of the film, it is Jus-tine's awareness that the planet Melancholia is heading towards Earth that leads to her increasingly 'erratic' behav-iour; the threat of extinction – the sense that time is running out – is what prompts her depressive spiral. But such a 'psy-chological' account is altogether too simplistic: it completely overlooks the politics of the situation.

Justine's depression is indicative of something deeply rotten in the bourgeois world within which she has been assigned a symbolic place. But her depression is not just a symptom of that world: it is also a means of effectuating a break from it – a tool of resistance and temporal disruption.

If it is part of the mechanism of capitalism to forbid recognition of the suffering it produces, then closely tied to this
is the view that discontent and unhappiness are themselves
moral faults – defects at the level of being itself.[33] It is no
surprise therefore that John and Claire, as upholders of status
quo normative values, demand that Justine remain happy at
all times. During one of her ghostly perambulations through
the house, Justine is ambushed by John, who delivers the
menacing lines: 'You better be goddam happy . . . Do you
have any idea of how much this party cost me? . . . A great
deal of money.' John is clearly unable to grasp that happiness
is not something that can be paid for in cash; nor is it a
temporal-affective state that an individual can simply 'choose'
to be in. 'The world of the happy', as Wittgenstein reminds
us, 'is quite different from that of the unhappy.'[34] But John's
happiness imperative merely provides Justine with further
evidence of what she already knows: that 'life on Earth is
evil' (as she later says to Claire) – meaning, specifically, the
social, familial, and economic forms of life that have now
come to dominate, along with their accompanying regimes of
'acceptable' and 'unacceptable' behaviour. What therefore
unfolds throughout the film is Justine's *great refusal*: her
uncompromising protest against the existing order of things,
and with this the construction of a new temporality – what
we might call (looking back to the previous chapter) the time
of the death drive.[35]

As we have already seen, the death drive is not a will
towards literal death. On the contrary, it refers to the uncanny
excess of life which undergirds the singularity of the subject.
While the death drive manifests itself in different ways, it
always entails a restructuring of the subject's place within the
symbolic order, and thus a restructuring of the symbolic
order as such. In the case of Justine, we might say that what

the death drive dissolves is an entire network of symbolic obligations, debts, and contracts. It is through the death drive, paradoxically, that Justine affirms life by *annihilating herself* as the 'good' daughter, sister, wife, and employee.[36]

To take just one revealing example: As a wedding gift from her boss Jack (Stellan Skarsgård), the head of an advertising agency, Justine receives a promotion – she is made art director of the firm. For Jack, however, all time is money, every day a workday, and so he spends the entire wedding reception trying to extract from Justine a 'tagline' for his latest advertising campaign.[37] Tiring of Jack's persistent demands, Justine eventually provides him with a slogan: *'nothing'*. Asked to elaborate on this enigmatic proposal, Justine responds as follows: 'Nothing is too much for you Jack. I hate you and your firm so deeply. I couldn't find the words to describe it. You are a despicable power-hungry little man, Jack.' What we find here, then, is the death drive operating as a dialectically subtractive drive. Justine clearly wants to get fired, to extinguish her career; but in so doing she is not acting out nihilistically. Her desire is simply to *begin again*, and in this specific case, to begin again outside the temporal order of 24/7 capitalism where, as she is reminded, 'she never stops working'. Of course, it is already too late to truly begin again – time has effectively run out, the earth and the human species are about to become extinct, as Justine may well be vaguely aware at this point – but this makes her act even more symbolically powerful. What it voices is a kind of militant paraphrase of what Martin Luther is reputed to have said when asked what he would do if the world would end tomorrow: 'I would plant an apple tree today.'[38]

Like the planet Melancholia that has managed to break free from the sun's gravitational pull, so Justine likewise goes rogue: freeing herself from her symbolic ties with others, exiting the orbit of the tightly time-governed structures of work, marriage, and family life.[39] While Justine is not (or at least not obviously) melancholic in the classic Freudian sense (she is not fixated on a lost, ego-supporting object), she might well be thought of as melancholic in a more Lacanian sense, especially if we foreground the role of the *Todestrieb*.[40] Three specific features stand out. First, she suffers not from the loss of a significant other, but rather from the *overbearing presence* of others and their relentless and suffocating demands. Second, she is disappointed not just with her specific spouse, boss, and family relations, but with *all* who would (potentially) occupy such roles. No one, we might say, could ever satisfy Justine's desire. And third, she confronts life from the position of someone who is, symbolically speaking, *already dead*.

But it is precisely this out-of-joint melancholic orientation that allows Justine to respond to the coming planetary catastrophe in a different way to those around her, to frame it in a different temporal register. In the second part of the film, when it becomes clear that Melancholia is on a collision course with Earth, subjectivities shift in the house, whose inhabitants are now reduced to Justine, Claire, John, and Leo. John, unable to maintain the idea of himself as an all-knowing Master, brings his own time to an end: retreating to the stables and overdosing on pills, leaving his wife and child to confront the apocalypse without him. Claire, thrown into an anxiety spiral by the rapidly approaching cosmic object, first tries to flee the estate with Leo, but when this plan fails she opts instead for the ultimate bourgeois solution: she asks Justine if the two of them might greet the end of the world with a 'glass of wine' on the 'outside terrace'. Justine reacts with disgust: 'You want us to gather on your terrace, sing a song, and have a glass of wine? . . . Do you know what I think of your plan? . . . Well, I think it is a piece of shit . . . Why don't we meet on the fucking toilet.' The time of the end will not therefore be Claire's time – a time of Chardonnay, candles, and cashmere blankets. Instead, Justine devotes her final hours to constructing for Leo a 'magic cave': a tepee-like structure made of stripped branches, which provides the frightened child with a comforting fictional bulwark against extinction.

This is not a move towards a sentimental ethics, but rather a radical act of care: the very antithesis of bourgeois 'coldness', which, in different ways, both of Leo's biological parents exhibit.[41] What enables Justine to act for the other in this way are two specific transformations. First, in seceding from her symbolic obligations, Justine stops being a child herself. To paraphrase Serge Leclaire, she succeeds in killing the fantasmatic image of the child inscribed in her by her parents, sister, and husband.[42] While this liberation leaves Justine bereft, languishing in a seemingly eternal twilight world, a later episode (which occurs early in the second part of the film) shifts the temporal gears once again, bringing her back to life in a new way.

In one of the most striking scenes of the film, Justine walks out of the house at night and reclines on a riverbank, her naked body bathed in the light emanating from the looming Melancholia. She is entirely consumed by the approaching planet; at one with it; annihilated and, at the same time, sensuously enlivened. After the encounter, she is utterly changed: her affect is lifted, her speech acquires a new clarity and purpose, and her relations with Claire and Leo resume in an entirely different key. Taking the incomprehensible object-void into herself – embracing the fact that the end has *already arrived* – is an act that triggers a new subjectivation for Justine.

To grasp the political significance of this encounter, we might begin by reading it alongside Adorno's description of the subject's experience of modernist art. In his late lectures on aesthetics (1958/9), Adorno argues that modernism has the power to remove the subject from 'the immediacy of a bad and questionable existence'. Where artistic experience is intensified and 'one becomes entirely one with the life of the work in the pulse, the rhythm of one's own life', one 'has the feeling of being lifted out . . . of transcending mere existence . . . of being freed'. These moments, Adorno says, are moments of 'being overwhelmed, of forgetting oneself . . . moments in which the subject annihilates itself and experiences happiness at this annihilation'.[43] This perfectly captures Justine's encounter with Melancholia; except that we will need to add one final step. It is only by experiencing the happiness – or better still the enjoyment (*jouissance*) – of annihilation that Justine is able to begin again from zero, that is, from the point of radical freedom.

This idea of beginning again from zero can also inform how we read the film's conclusion, which, in a neat dialectical twist, is already staged at its start. During the final shot of the prologue, when Earth and Melancholia fatally collide, what we see resembles a microscopic image of insemination. Extinction here is thus transfigured into (pro)creation.

Almost two hours later, at the end of the film, when Earth and all its inhabitants have been wiped out, we are presented with a black screen that endures for in excess of ten seconds. All seems corpsed. Until that is (and surely this cannot be a coincidence) we are reminded of Kazimir Malevich's modernist painting *The Black Square* (1915) – Malevich being the artist whose work Justine covers over in a display of art books in Part One of the film, when she is still not yet ready to tarry with the prospect of extinction. While this iconic painting (literally a black square on a white ground) continues to raise important aesthetic and philosophical questions – Is it matter? Is it spirit? Is it silence? Is it noise? Is it laughter? Is it scorn? – what the painting 'is', ultimately, is *nothing*. For Malevich, however, nothing is not a final end point, but rather the zero-level from which creation itself emerges.[44] As he puts it in his 'Suprematist Manifesto' (1916): 'I have transformed myself in the zero of form and through zero have reached creation, that is, Suprematism, the new painterly realism – non-objective creation.'[45]

Embodying the dialectical logic of the film's conclusion, Justine, we might say, is intuitively aware that 'it is from zero, in zero, that the true movement of being begins'.[46] She reaches nothing (symbolic self-murder, opening herself up to the real of planetary catastrophe) not to stop there, but in order to go *beyond nothing*: to unleash, in Malevich's words, 'the joy of new things'.[47] While John and Claire both cling tightly to their closed world, built around the bourgeois ideals of happiness and wealth, Justine stands for the undoing of that world, its erasure from within. Far from simply desiring death or taking a perverse delight in the spectacle of absolute destruction, Justine is instead a forceful reminder of that most radical of modernist propositions: *nothing is the force that renovates the world*.[48]

If all of this sounds revolutionary, then that is because it is. Except, of course, that Justine is a revolutionary without a clear political programme, and, it goes without saying, without a possible future. Let us therefore delve further into how this position might acquire a concrete and active shape, outside of the realm of fiction.

Revolutionary Decreation

I.

In her posthumously published notebooks, the philosopher and political activist Simone Weil writes that 'we participate in the creation of the world by decreating ourselves'.[49] This is Weil in her mystic rather than Marxist mode.[50] 'The object of all our efforts', she says, 'is to *become nothing.*' Becoming nothing – 'empty[ing] ourselves of the false divinity with which we were born' – is necessary 'in order to liberate a *tied up* energy, in order to possess an energy which is free and capable of understanding the true relationships of things'.[51] Weil's project of *decreation* ('an undoing of the creature in us', as the poet Anne Carson neatly puts it) aims at removing or eliminating the self (the all-consuming 'I') which, for Weil, ultimately stands in the way of our communion with God.[52]

Strip away the theological language here and one finds striking parallels with the practice of psychoanalysis. Decreation as a mode of self-undoing might be another way of describing Lacan's notion of '*subjective destitution*':[53] the point where the subject, at the end of analysis, having traversed the fantasy and liquidated the transference, loses its (imaginary) status as a subject and is reduced to a kind of 'excremental remainder'.[54] This end point, however, also marks (potentially at least) a moment of radical transformation: one in which the analysand embarks upon the *passage* to becoming an analyst. Lacan articulates this movement in the following terms:

> shouldn't the true termination of an analysis – and by that
> I mean the kind that prepares you to become an analyst –
> in the end confront the one who undergoes it with the

reality of the human condition? [This is] the state in which man is in that relationship to himself which is his own death ... At the end of a training analysis the subject should reach and should know the domain and the experience of absolute disarray.[55]

Weil's decreation and Lacan's subjective destitution are both, then, dialectical notions of *self-extinction*: the subject enters a 'zone of daring' and experiences its own symbolic death as a necessary part of a creative process of rebirth, of beginning again at the end.

To this list of dialectical notions of self-extinction, we need finally to add Marx's theory of revolution. In the Introduction to his critique of Hegel's *Philosophy of Right*, Marx asks, 'Where, then, is the positive possibility of German emancipation?' He responds to his own question with a breathtaking piece of political and philosophical prose:

Our answer: in the formation of a class with *radical* chains, a class in civil society that is not of civil society, an estate that is the dissolution of all estates, a sphere of society having a universal character because of its universal suffering and claiming no *particular right* because no *particular wrong* but *unqualified wrong* is perpetuated on it; a sphere that can claim no *historical* title but only a *human* title; a sphere that does not stand partially opposed to the consequences, but totally opposed to the premises of the German political system; a sphere, finally, that cannot emancipate itself without emancipating itself from all the other spheres of society, thereby emancipating them; a sphere, in short, that is the *complete loss* of humanity and can only redeem itself through the *total redemption of humanity*. This dissolution of society existing as a particular estate is the *proletariat*.[56]

Marx's perspective here is modernist through and through. The proletariat is the embodiment of suffering and emptiness – *the complete loss of humanity*. So how then to bring about *'the total redemption of humanity'* (to use Marx's own deliberately theological phrase)? The answer, simply put, is *revolutionary decreation*. As Lukács neatly summarizes in his *History and Class Consciousness* (1922): *'The proletariat only perfects itself by annihilating and transcending itself, by creating the classless society through the successful conclusion of its own class struggle.'*[57] But this struggle isn't simply a struggle against an external enemy; rather, it is equally a 'struggle of the proletariat *against itself*: against the devastating and degrading effects of the capitalist system upon its class consciousness. The proletariat will only have won the real victory when it has overcome these effects within itself.'[58]

II.

It will, however, be necessary to add a number of important footnotes to Marx and Lukács. First, the struggle of the self *against itself* needs to be cast in the correct light. The difficulty of such a process inheres not only in the immense task of decoupling from capitalist desire, but also in the fact that the subject's *full actualization*, which the idea of redeeming humanity clearly implies, will always necessarily fail. It will fail not because revolutions always necessarily fail (as cynical reason might have us believe), but rather because alienation is itself a *constitutive feature of human subjectivity*: one rooted in the fact that the subject is condemned to see itself emerge only in the field of the Other – that is to say, in language which is never the subject's own.[59] Any attempt to locate revolutionary subjectivity will therefore need to begin by acknowledging that there can be no final 'transcendence' of alienation, no 'complete return of man to himself', no point at which 'essence' and 'existence' are harmoniously united.⁶⁰ The divided human subject – the subject who is, to some extent, *always* a stranger and an enemy to itself – is the basic ontological unit of politics.

But all of this only makes the activity of revolutionary decreation even more urgent. For what is annihilated is one's existence as a permanently exploited being, 'reduced', as Lukács puts it, 'to an isolated particle and fed into an alien system'.⁶¹ What revolution therefore negates is what we might call *surplus alienation*: it shatters capitalism's 'natural laws' and its 'rational' social order, opening up the space for new ways of being in the world, new realms of meaning. In light of this, we might therefore re-imagine the redemption of humanity in the following way: a future of *liberated, classless neurotics* – neurotic because that just is the basic structure of human speaking beings – who, no longer subject to the mute compulsion of life-devouring market logic, are now able to realize actual freedom and genuine creativity in both their everyday actions and their collective relations with others.⁶²

Here we are reminded of Jameson's call for a 'utopia of misfits and oddballs', 'in which the constraints for uniformization and conformity have been removed, and human beings grow wild like plants in a state of nature'.⁶³ Communism, we might say, is what allows true singularities to emerge. Such a state of liberated sociality will, quite clearly, coincide with the emergence of new temporalities beyond those determined by the current rhythms of accumulation. Rather than the frantic time of endless flows, feeds, and streams – and beyond the mundane crisis time announced by tipping points, climate deadlines, and doomsday clocks – we might recall Justine's desire for sleep (perchance to dream) in *Melancholia*, alongside Adorno's image of a utopian time, where the subject, free from the 'frantic bustle' of 'operating' and 'planning', can now enjoy simply *lying on water and looking peacefully at the sky*.[64]

Of course, we cannot say exactly how temporalities will unfold in the context of an emancipated society. Nevertheless, in addition to the hints just provided, we might also point to the time of the psychoanalytic encounter as another kind of partial blueprint. For the time of analysis is a time when the tyranny of clock time is suspended; when free association is the goal; when the unconscious (which, for Freud, knows 'no time') is allowed to speak, enabling the emergence of new truths; and when the past is no longer seen as merely scattered behind us, but is brought fully into existence in the here and now. The time of analysis is the temporality of another scene: a tangled drama of desire, transference, and repetition, whose rhythms are constantly shifting. This is not a time of breathless immediacy when one is implored to 'do something' and 'act now'. Instead, it is a time when one is simply *given time* to engage in a process of reinventing what it means to be a human subject in the world.

III.

In terms of what might be expected from a politically transformed society, however, we will need to add another note of caution. Such a society will not be free from sad passions.[65] That is to say, it will not be free from envy, resentment, or a whole host of other affective conflicts.[66] Human beings are, to repeat an earlier phrase, *freaks of nature*: constitutively divided subjects, who cannot but maintain an eccentric relationship with their own enjoyment.[67] Indeed, enjoyment forever oscillates between surplus and lack: an overbearing 'too much' and a disappointing 'too little'. It is in this context that the other is encountered as *troublesome*: as one who blocks our enjoyment, disturbingly enjoys more than we do (or in ways that we do not), or threatens to steal our enjoyment from us completely. This antagonistic relationship is not one that a new politics can simply 'fix'; nor will such a politics be able to make of our enjoyment something wholly 'rational', as if a transformation of *what is* would coincide with a termination of the unconscious itself.

What a liberated society can bring about, however, are two things. First, a restructuring of the symbolic coordinates within which enjoyment itself plays out. This would (potentially at least) open up a new language-game of enjoyment: one tied to the project of collective self-emancipation – a project which, as Marx reminds us, needs to be constantly repeated. Indeed, revolutionary repetition (perpetually beginning again) produces its own mode of political enjoyment. As we read in 'The Eighteenth Brumaire':

Proletarian revolutions . . . engage in perpetual self-criticism, always stopping in their own tracks; they return to what is apparently complete in order to begin it anew, and deride with savage brutality the inadequacies, weak points and pitiful aspects of their first attempts; they seem to strike down their adversary, only to have him draw new powers from the earth and rise against them once more with the strength of a giant; again and again they draw back from the prodigious scope of their own aims, until a situation is created which makes impossible any reversion, and circumstances themselves cry out:

Hic Rhodus, hic salta!
Hier ist die Rose, hier tanze!
[Here is the rose, dance here!][68]

The second thing an emancipated future might produce is a transformation of our understanding of the sad passions themselves. To take envy as an example: capitalism exploits and manipulates envy, using it to drive competition and consumption, while at the same time designating it as a 'destructive' emotion that we have a duty to overcome. Turning this around, however, we might say that envy should instead be brought out into the open and its revelatory aspects fully explored.[69] What provokes envy is not the 'thing' that the other possesses – money, intelligence, beauty, professional success – but rather the image of the other enjoying through the thing.[70] To paraphrase Kant, we have a propensity to view the enjoyment of the other with distress, because the scene of the other enjoying appears to indicate a plenitude or completion that we, by comparison, lack.[71]

Only a new dialectical approach to envy can invert this fantasy. The other may well have something that we do not have, but this does not grant them access to a special kind of unfettered enjoyment; they are, in reality, just as lacking as we are ourselves. But knowing this does not enable us to completely free ourselves of envy, which remains a constitutive component of human desire. Elevating this situation to the necessary next level requires the intervention of radical politics. Moving beyond the utopian fictions of communal harmony and neighbourly love, such a politics can create the material conditions for a new form of enjoyment: an enjoyment of the very *ontological glitch* out of which envy and self-alienation emerge, but where this glitch is now experienced from the de-individualized perspective of class struggle itself.

This would be a genuine instance of beginning again: a dismantling of the current social arrangement that goes hand in hand with a transformation of the subject's self-understanding – something to be truly enjoyed as it opens, via the unconscious, onto the unknown.

Saints or Barbarians?

Today's radical politics needs to avoid false promises. Emancipatory change will not bring about the subject's lasting satisfaction, unperturbed contentment, or enduring happiness. It will not usher in complete libidinal liberation, a joyful encounter with one's 'authentic self', or a final alleviation of human suffering. Abolishing private property and the wage relation won't allow us to give anxiety the slip, free us from the strange compulsion to repeat painful and traumatic events, or enable us to simply ignore the cruel demands of the superego. We are reminded of Hamm's exhortation in *Endgame*: 'Use your head, can't you, use your head, you're on Earth, there's no cure for that!'

To put the point another way: capitalism may well end, but this won't be the end of our problems. Nevertheless, the fight for a more liveable existence – a new collective form of life – remains *the* political fight. But here the crucial question inevitably returns: how, specifically, might we move beyond the damaged life of the present?

In *Television*, a series of interviews from 1974, Lacan suggests a possible 'way out of capitalist discourse'.[72] He links the figure of the analyst with the figure of the saint. By this comparison, Lacan does not mean that the analyst demonstrates the saintly virtues of compassion or charity (*caritas*). Rather, the analyst's saintliness involves them acting as trash (*déchet*) in the analytic process, becoming waste, allowing the analysand to take them as object *a* – the *object cause* of their own desire.[73] The analyst-as-saint does not enter into the spirit of capitalism: he or she does not produce anything of value for the system (certainly not 'efficient' or 'well-adapted' subjects); nor do they situate themselves within the consumerist logic framed by 'demand' (the only demand that the analyst responds to is the patient's demand that analysis might begin). As Lacan therefore concludes: 'The more saints, the more laughter; that's my principle, to wit, the way out of capitalist discourse – which will not constitute progress if it happens only for some.'[74]

This is indeed a strange politics. On the one hand, Lacan seems to be advocating a thoroughgoing Marxist universalism – the emancipation of one requires the emancipation of all. At the same time, the saintly exit from capitalism is clearly reserved only for a select few – a few, we might add, whose imagined distance from the system makes them all the more complicit in it. As Adorno reminds us, there is no way of simply sidestepping our involvement with capitalism. Whoever thinks they stand aloof 'is as much entangled as the active participant'; distance from capitalism is itself a capitalist fantasy.[75] Saintliness, we might say, therefore ends up unwittingly serving what it protests, reproducing the very illusions for which it takes itself to be the cure.

What is required, then, is not an 'exit' from 'capitalist discourse', but rather a psychoanalytically informed politics that aims at overcoming capitalism as such.

In a short text from 1933 entitled 'Experience and Poverty', Walter Benjamin presents the notion of 'positive barbarism'. Eerily evoking our present moment, Benjamin says that with the tremendous developments of new technologies 'a completely new poverty' descends on humankind: a 'poverty of human experience in general'.[76] This poverty is characterized by excess rather than lack: a suffocating abundance of new ideas and styles that produce a feeling of generalized exhaustion; a sense that, from culture to people, everything has now been 'devoured'.[77] For Benjamin, however, this situation is not simply to be lamented: the condition of experiential poverty is precisely what challenges the subject to *begin again*. And this is the dialectical starting point for his new concept of *positive barbarism*:

> For what does poverty of experience do for the barbarian? It forces him to start from scratch; to make a new start; to make a little go a long way; to begin with a little and build up further . . . Among the great creative spirits, there have always been the inexorable ones who begin by clearing a tabula rasa.[78]

Benjamin goes on to define the new barbarian as one who demonstrates 'a total absence of illusion about the age and at the same time an unlimited commitment to it'.[79] Rejecting all nostalgic attachments to the past, the new barbarian is the 'naked [subject] of the contemporary world who lies screaming like a newborn babe in the dirty diapers of the present'.[80]

The new barbarian is therefore the exact opposite of the saint: while the latter clings to an idea of bourgeois purity, the former plunges into the stinking filth of the here and now. The terrain of political struggle, as Benjamin implicitly acknowledges, has shifted. The question facing us is no longer 'socialism or barbarism?' We are in fact already *in* barbarism, which is to say, the final (although potentially long-lasting) death throes of capitalist 'civilization'. What is thus required is a new dialectical politics that can bring about the negation of this *civilized barbarism*, a mimetic politics that adapts itself to the barbarous world in order to explode it from within.

The new barbarian is allied to what Benjamin calls, in another short text, the destructive character. The latter, like the former, is in the business of dirtying their hands. The destructive character, Benjamin remarks,

knows only one watchword: make room. And only one
activity: clearing away . . . Where others encounter walls
or monuments, there, too, he sees a way. But because he
sees a way everywhere, he has to clear things from it everywhere. Not only by brute force; sometimes by the most
refined means . . . What exists he reduces to rubble – not
for the sake of the rubble, but for that of the way leading
through it.[81]

Benjamin's point here is extremely clear: the new, both experientially and materially, can come about only through a fully
accomplished destruction. Against capitalist destruction,
what is needed is the 'rejuvenating' and 'cheerful' destruction
of capitalism itself.

Let us make no mistake: 'That things are "status quo" *is*
the catastrophe . . . Hell is not something that awaits us, but
this life here and now.'[82] Benjamin's brutal, interruptive, and
reconstructive thinking is therefore precisely what we need
to inherit today. What is required, we might say, is a *new
political barbarism*, a barbarism that can actively confront
what our 'civilized society' delivers up: accelerating climate
change, ecological catastrophe, endless war, untold economic
misery, and a deliberate destruction of the social bond ('there
is no such thing as society').

This new political barbarism will be first and foremost a
collective politics: one that uses whatever it can (strikes,
sabotage, art, philosophy, psychoanalysis, technology) to
create the conditions for beginning again beyond the existing order of things. Second, reading the repetition of the
'bar' in barbarism, it will be a politics of the barred (or
split) subject ($); that is to say, a generative politics of the
death drive – one that avoids the fantasy of complete dis-
alienation. And third, it will be a politics of language. While

capitalism treats language as an instrumental tool for describing the world, the new political barbarism will mobilize language in the service of class struggle, of changing reality. We are here reminded of Althusser's powerful statement: 'words are . . . weapons, explosives or tranquilizers and even poisons. Occasionally, the whole class struggle may be summed up in the struggle for one word against another word . . . The philosophical fight over words is part of the political fight.'[83]

It is by rupturing the omnipresent present – the present as stuckness – that politics is able to bring the past back into being, to retroactively awaken the blocked possibilities of previous failed revolutionary attempts. In this respect, the new political barbarism will strive towards what Marx calls *the conscious completion of old work*: the actualization of the radical past through its repetition and fulfilment in the here and now. But key to this new dialectical politics, as Benjamin reminds us, is that it is carried out 'with a laugh' – which is to say, a *barbaric laugh*. And this, of course, returns us to Lacan's figure of the saint, who likewise sees laughter as punctuating the political break. But why should laughter, of all things, play such an important role here?

In the first volume of *Capital*, Marx tells the story of the laughing capitalist: the one who can hardly believe his good luck when he realizes how easy it is to appropriate surplus value. The capitalist purchases a commodity (labour power), and by exploiting this commodity, by putting it to use, the value it 'creates' is 'double' what he pays for it.[84] It is as if by a kind of magical transformation something is conjured out of nothing. 'Our capitalist', Marx says, 'foresaw this situation, and that was the cause of his laughter.'[85] Marx therefore sees a direct link between excess within the sphere of capitalist economy (surplus value [*Mehrwert*]) and excess within the sphere of psychic economy (laughter as a mode of what Lacan will later call surplus enjoyment [*Mehrlust*]).

But while the capitalist laughs to himself, believing that his 'trick' of appropriating surplus value can go on indefinitely, his demonic chuckling always threatens to trigger something in the collective: a realization that the existing state of affairs is but a sick joke, at once loathsome and ridiculous. To paraphrase Marx: to come to see the present world as risible is to arrive at a point at which we can begin to consider 'happily' taking our leave of it.[86] This, we might say, is the moment at which barbaric laughter comes to be heard. Laughter, as Benjamin points out, is 'the most international and the most revolutionary emotion of the masses'. It is also a new starting point for thought: 'convulsions of the diaphragm generally offer better chances for thought than convulsions of the soul'.[87] Barbaric laughter thus signals the moment when the collective arrives at a new beginning, a zero-point. Such laughter shatters the familiar psychic landscape and explodes the established temporal order. It is an exemplary instance of subjective destitution: one 'cracks up', 'breaks down', 'collapses', 'chokes', 'splits one's sides', or simply 'dies'. But the explosion of barbaric laughter in the body simultaneously reconnects one with others, filling life to the bursting point with new possibilities.

A wonderful example of this can be found in a scene in Ernst Lubitsch's 1939 romantic comedy *Ninotchka*. The titular character, played by Greta Garbo, is a Soviet special envoy dispatched to Paris to fix a trade deal bungled by three of her male comrades. One lunchtime she goes to eat alone in a workers' café, where she is pursued by Count Leon d'Algout (Melvyn Douglas), an aristocrat who is trying to seduce her. In a bid to break through Ninotchka's hard communist shell, Leon tells a number of jokes, all of which fall embarrassingly flat. Flustered by his failure to elicit even a smile, Leon begins rocking nervously on his chair. Suddenly the chair topples backwards, and Leon crashes to the ground taking down the table behind him. Witnessing this, all the workers in the café erupt into raucous laughter; when the camera switches to Ninotchka, she too is howling uncontrollably, her body convulsing, her eyes filled with tears, her head thrown backwards, her hands banging on the table in joyful abandon. What we encounter here, then, is a kind of infectious universalism: a truly barbaric laughter that forges a new collectivity while, at the same time, evoking a future sociality in which enjoyment is no longer tethered to surplus value.

On a standard reading of the film, Ninotchka's fall into laughter is part of her fall for the West, her fall into capitalist desire. But precisely the opposite is the case. While she falls out of love with Soviet state socialism (and into love with Leon), she never stops being a true revolutionary. Indeed, her break with Stalinism – signalled by her laughter – arguably makes her an even better Marxist, more able to win over others to the cause. 'Ever since you met that Bolshevik lady', Leon's butler remarks, shortly after the café scene, 'I've noticed a distinct change in you, sir . . . It was with great amazement that I found a copy of Karl Marx's *Capital* on your night table.' Later in the film, during an evening out at a high-end Parisian establishment, a jovial Ninotchka begins spreading 'communist propaganda' in the lady's powder room, 'inciting the attendants to go on strike', much to the horror of the manager and the other patrons. And how does Leon at one point refer to his new communist love? 'My barbaric Ninotchka.' Her slogan might well be: *Neither Paris nor Moscow, but a new international barbarism – let things begin again, and begin again with laughter.*

Something along these lines should be our own slogan today.

Acknowledgements

I'd like to thank the following people, whose generous contributions – in the form of readings, conversations and comments – helped make this a better book than it would otherwise have been: Maria Balaska, Peter Buse, Daniela Caselli, Alex Callinicos, Howard Caygill, Vincent Dachy, Rohit Goel, Sacha Golob, Gregg Horowitz, Dany Nobus, Benjamin Noys, Hans-Ulrich Obrist, Frank Ruda, and Alenka Zupančič. I am also grateful to Kaye Cain-Nielsen (at *e-flux journal*) and Jeremy Gilbert (at *New Formations*) for facilitating the publication of early versions of some of the chapters.

At Verso, I could not have wished for a better editor than Leo Hollis: he knew exactly what I wanted to do, right from the very start, and got me to do it better.

Special thanks to both of my parents, Bernie and Phil Ware, for their continued support; and also to Lucie Ware and Joe Hage. And last — because always first — to Sarah, with whom I really did begin again at the end. Her love and laughter make everything possible.

Notes

1 A Dialectics of Extinction

1. Immanuel Kant, 'The End of All Things', in *Religion and Rational Theology*, trans. Allen W. Wood and George Di Giovanni (Cambridge: Cambridge University Press, 1996), p. 227.

2. Friedrich Nietzsche, 'On the Truth and Lies in a Nonmoral Sense', in *Philosophy and Truth: Selections from Nietzsche's Notebooks of the Early 1870s*, trans. Daniel Breazeale (New York: Humanity Books, 1979), p. 79. For an alternative reading of Nietzsche's fable in relation to extinction, see Ray Brassier, *Nihil Unbound: Enlightenment and Extinction* (London: Palgrave, 2007), ch. 7.

3. See Domenico Losurdo, *Nietzsche, the Aristocratic Rebel: Intellectual Biography and Critical Balance-Sheet*, trans. Gregor Benton (Chicago: Haymarket Books, 2021), p. 27. The physicist Rudolph Clausius coined the term 'heat-death' in 1865. Clausius observes that when the universe attains the condition at which its entropy reaches a maximum, no further change can take place and the universe will 'be in a state of unchanging death'. See P. M. Harman, *Energy, Force, and Matter: The Conceptual Developments of Nineteenth-Century Physics* (London: Cambridge University Press, 1982), p. 65.

4. See Losurdo, *Nietzsche, the Aristocratic Rebel*, ch. 1.

5. Judith Butler, 'Creating an Inhabitable World for Humans Means Dismantling Rigid Forms of Individuality', *Time*, 21 April 2021.

6. See Slavoj Žižek, 'Last Exit to Socialism', *Jacobin*, 21 July 2021.

7. Adrian Johnston, *Prolegomena to Any Future Materialism*, vol. 2, *A Weak Nature Alone* (Evanston, IL: Northwestern University Press, 2019), p. 26.

8. Slavoj Žižek, *Tarrying with the Negative: Kant, Hegel, and the Critique of Ideology* (Durham, NC: Duke University Press, 1993), p. 30.

9. G. W. F. Hegel, *Phenomenology of Spirit*, trans. A. V. Miller (Oxford: Oxford University Press, 1977), p. 21.

10. Jacques Lacan, *The Seminar of Jacques Lacan, Book XI: The Four Fundamental Concepts of Psychoanalysis*, trans. Alan Sheridan (New York: W. W. Norton & Co., 1981), pp. 263ff.

11. Louis Althusser, *The Spectre of Hegel: Early Writings*, trans. G. M. Goshgarian (London: Verso, 2014), p. 173.

12. Russell Sbriglia and Slavoj Žižek, 'Subject Matters', in *Subject Lessons: Hegel, Lacan and the Future of Materialism*, ed. Russell Sbriglia and Slavoj Žižek (Evanston, IL: Northwestern University Press, 2020), p. 13.

13. The idea of a non-rapport or non-relation with nature draws on Lacan's expression: 'there's no such thing as a sexual relation' (*il n'y a pas de rapport sexuel*). Jacques Lacan, *The Seminar of Jacques Lacan, Book XX: Encore, 1972–1973*, trans. Bruce Fink (London: W. W. Norton & Co., 1999), p. 59ff.

14. Kant, 'The End of All Things', pp. 224–5.

15. Immanuel Kant, 'Conjectural Beginning of Human History' (1786), in *Anthropology, History and Education*, trans. Mary Gregor et al. (Cambridge: Cambridge University Press, 2007), pp. 164–5.

16. Jacques Lacan, 'Lituraterre', trans. Dany Nobus, *Continental Philosophy Review* 46(1), 2013, pp. 327–34 (emphasis added).

17. See Bertolt Brecht, 'Saint Joan of the Stockyards', in *Collected Plays: Three*, trans. Ralph Manheim (London: Methuen, 1998), p. 285. See also Theodor Adorno, *Negative Dialectics*, trans. E. B. Ashton (London: Routledge, 2004), p. 366.

18. Alenka Zupančič, 'The End of Ideology, the Ideology of the End', *South Atlantic Quarterly* 119(4), 2020, pp. 833–44 (833).

19. Ibid., p. 834. Here we are also reminded of Fredric Jameson's famous remark: 'It seems to be easier for us today to imagine the thoroughgoing deterioration of the earth and of nature than the breakdown of late capitalism.' Fredric Jameson, *The Seeds of Time* (New York: Columbia University Press, 1994), p. xii. See also Slavoj Žižek, 'The Spectre of Ideology', in *Mapping Ideology* (London: Verso, 1994), p. 1.

20. On the temporality of the 'new chronic' condition, see Eric Cazdyn, *The Already Dead: The New Time of Politics, Culture, and Illness* (Durham, NC: Duke University Press, 2012), pp. 13–98.

21. George Caffentzis, *In Letters of Blood and Fire: Work, Machines, and the Crisis of Capitalism* (Oakland, CA: PM Press, 2013), p. 12.

22. See Jacques Lacan, *L'insu que sait . . .*, Seminar XXIV 1976–77 (session of 17 May 1977), trans. Cormac Gallagher, Jacques Lacan in Ireland, lacaninireland.com.

23. According to the discourse of the anthropocene, the only kind of intervention that human beings can now make is to act as 'planetary managers' overseeing 'large-scale geo-engineering projects' in order to '"optimize" climate'. See Paul J. Crutzen, 'The Anthropocene: Geology of Mankind', *Nature* 415, January 2000.

24. Jacques Lacan, *The Seminar of Jacques Lacan, Book XI: The Four Fundamental Concepts of Psychoanalysis*, trans. Alan Sheridan (New York: W. W. Norton & Co., 1981), pp. 17ff.

25. Gilles Deleuze, 'Coldness and Cruelty', in *Masochism* (New York: Zone Books, 1991), pp. 81–94.

26. This alternative (counter-Deleuzean) view of masochism – which, with some modifications, would seem to perfectly capture the subject-position of the XR activist – is theoretically derived from Lacan. See Jacques Lacan, *The Seminar of Jacques*

Lacan, Book X: Anxiety, trans. A. R. Price (Cambridge: Polity Press, 2014), pp. 105–7ff.

27. Here we can paraphrase Lacan: *What you aspire to as extinction rebels is a master. You will get one!* See Jacques Lacan, *The Seminar of Jacques Lacan, Book XVII: The Other Side of Psychoanalysis*, trans. Russell Grigg (London: W. W. Norton & Co., 1991), p. 207.

28. As Jacques-Alain Miller points out: *père-version* 'is untranslatable, made up of *père*, father, and *version*. It implies *a turning to the father, a call to the father*, which is also perhaps a very profound reminder that perversion is, in no sense, a subversion.' Jacques-Alain Miller, 'Perversion', in *Reading Seminars I and II: Lacan's Return to Freud*, ed. Richard Feldstein et al. (Albany: State University of New York Press, 1996), p. 308 (emphasis in original).

29. Franz Kafka, 'Give It Up', in *Franz Kafka: The Complete Stories* (New York: Schocken Books, 1971), p. 456.

30. Alain Badiou, *Philosophy for Militants*, trans. Bruno Bosteels (London: Verso, 2012), p. 6.

31. Ibid., p. 17.

32. Ibid., p. 16.

33. Ludwig Wittgenstein, *Culture and Value*, trans. Peter Winch (Chicago: University of Chicago Press, 1984), pp. 48–9.

34. Gertrude Stein, 'Reflections on the Atomic Bomb' (1946), *Yale Poetry Review* (1947), writing.upenn.edu.

35. Ludwig Wittgenstein, *Culture and Value: A Selection from the Posthumous Remains*, trans. Peter Winch (Oxford: Blackwell, 1998), p. 56. It is worth recalling Wittgenstein's politics at this point. He was much further to the left than Russell or Einstein. Among his closest friends were George Thompson (the Marxist professor of classics), Maurice Dobb (the Marxist economist), Rush Rhees (a Trotskyite, who later became one of Wittgenstein's translators), Piero Sraffa (the great Marxist economist,

close friend of Antonio Gramsci, and the person to whom Wittgenstein effectively dedicated his later work), Roy Pascal (who edited an English edition of the first and third parts of Marx's *The German Ideology*), Fania Pascal (a Marxist who taught him Russian), and Nikolai Bakhtin (elder brother of the famed Mikhail, and the person to whom Wittgenstein first read his *Philosophical Investigations*). Wittgenstein's politics are, to be sure, radically *uneven*. That said, he described himself as 'a communist at heart', criticized his close friend Frank Ramsey for being a 'bourgeois thinker', and his work is littered with genuinely materialist philosophical-political insights, such as the following: 'The sickness of a time is cured by an alteration in the mode of life of human beings, and it [is] possible for the sickness of philosophical problems to get cured *only* through a changed mode of thought and of life, not through a medicine invented by an individual.' See Ludwig Wittgenstein, *Remarks on the Foundations of Mathematics*, trans. G. E. M. Anscombe (Oxford: Blackwell, 1989), p. 132.

36. Wittgenstein, *Culture and Value: A Selection* (1998 edition), p. 64.

37. Wittgenstein, *Culture and Value* (1984 edition), p. 63; and Ludwig Wittgenstein, *Philosophical Investigations*, trans. G. E. M. Anscombe (Oxford: Blackwell, 2001), p. x.

38. Theodor Adorno and Max Horkheimer, *Dialectic of Enlightenment*, trans. John Cumming (London: Verso, 1997), p. 3.

39. Günther Anders, 'Theses for the Atomic Age', *Massachusetts Review* 3(2), 1962, pp. 493–505 (496).

40. Ibid.

41. Günther Anders, 'Reflections on the H Bomb', *Dissent* 3(2), 1956, pp. 146–55 (146).

42. Ibid. (emphasis added).

43. Anders, 'Theses for the Atomic Age', p. 493.

44. Ibid., p. 498.

45. The phrase is from Jean-Pierre Dupuy, one of Anders's most sophisticated readers. See, for example, Jean-Pierre Dupuy, 'The Precautionary Principle and Enlightened Doomsaying: Rational Choice before the Apocalypse', *Occasion: Interdisciplinary Studies in the Humanities* 1(1), 2009, pp. 1–13.

46. Cited in Jean-Pierre Dupuy, *The Mark of the Sacred*, trans. M. B. DeBevoise (Stanford, CA: Stanford University Press, 2013), p. 203.

47. Ibid., p. 204.

48. For Dupuy's reference to enlightened doomsaying as a 'ruse', see, for example, Jean-Pierre Dupuy, *A Short Treatise on the Metaphysics of Tsunamis*, trans. M. B. DeBevoise (East Lansing: Michigan State University Press, 2015).

49. On the fear of a breakdown that has already occurred, see D. W. Winnicott, 'Fear of Breakdown', *International Review of Psychoanalysis* 1, 1974, pp. 103–7.

50. Walter Benjamin, 'Paralipomena to *On the Concept of History*', in *Selected Writings*, vol. 4, *1938–1940*, ed. Howard Eiland and Michael Jennings (Cambridge, MA: Belknap Press of Harvard University Press, 2003), p. 402.

51. Ibid., p. 170.

52. Adorno, *Negative Dialectics*, p. 320.

53. G. W. F. Hegel, *Lectures on the Philosophy of World History*, trans. H. B. Nisbet (Cambridge: Cambridge University Press, 1984), pp. 29, 52, 65.

54. Adorno, *Negative Dialectics*, p. 320.

55. Theodor Adorno, 'Progress', in *Critical Models*, ed. Henry Pickford (New York: Columbia University Press, 2005), p. 144.

56. Adorno, *Negative Dialectics*, p. 320.

57. See also Franco 'Bifo' Berardi, *Breathing: Chaos and Poetry* (South Pasadena, CA: Semiotext(e), 2018).

58. Adorno, 'Progress', p. 145.

59. Ibid., p. 144. See also Theodor Adorno, *History and Freedom: Lectures 1964–1965*, trans. Rodney Livingstone (London: Polity Press, 2006), pp. 116, 118, 123, 143.

60. Friedrich Hölderlin, 'Patmos', in *Selected Poems and Fragments*, trans. Michael Hamburger (London: Penguin, 1998), p. 231. For an important critique of the 'Hölderlin paradigm', see Slavoj Žižek, *Absolute Recoil: Towards a New Foundation of Dialectical Materialism* (London: Verso, 2015), pp. 344ff. See also Mladen Dolar, 'The Endgame of Aesthetics: From Hegel to Beckett', *Problemi International* 3(3), 2019, pp. 185–214. I fully concur with these criticisms. There is no simple redemptive reversal of the worst, as I make clear in the conclusion to this chapter and throughout.

61. Sigmund Freud, 'Thoughts for the Times on War and Death', in *The Standard Edition of the Complete Works of Sigmund Freud*, vol. 14, *1914–1916*, trans. James Strachey (London: Vintage, 2001), p. 291. Hereafter all references to Freud's writings will appear in the notes as *SE* followed by a volume number.

62. Maurice Blanchot, 'The Apocalypse Is Disappointing', in *Friendship*, trans. Elizabeth Rottenberg (Stanford, CA: Stanford University Press, 1997), pp. 101–3. If anything, Blanchot is too politically reticent in his treatment of Jaspers. The latter was a vehement anti-Marxist, who participated in the founding conference of the Congress for Cultural Freedom (CCF), a CIA-backed anti-communist group that operated in Europe, North America, Asia, Africa, Latin America, and Australia between 1950 and 1979.

63. Ibid., pp. 105–7.

64. Alenka Zupančič, 'The Apocalypse Is (Still) Disappointing', *S: Journal of the Circle of Lacanian Ideology Critique* 10 & 11, 2017–18, pp. 16–30 (28).

65. Louis Althusser, *History and Imperialism: Writings, 1963–1986*, trans. G. M. Goshgarian (London: Polity Press, 2020), p. 50.

66. Ernst Bloch, *On Karl Marx* (London: Verso, 2018), p. 44.

2 Extinction Episodes: From the Sublime to the Demonic

1. Ludwig Wittgenstein, *Culture and Value*, ed. G. H. Von Wright (London: Blackwell, 1998), p. 5.

2. Judite Nozes, ed., *The Lisbon Earthquake of 1755: Some British Eye-Witness Accounts* (Lisbon: British Historical Society of Portugal, 1987), p. 36.

3. Johann Wolfgang von Goethe, *Truth and Poetry: From My Own Life*, vol. 1 (Cambridge: Cambridge University Press, 2013), p. 31.

4. Theodor Adorno, *Negative Dialectics*, trans. E. B. Ashton (London: Routledge, 2004), p. 361.

5. Voltaire, 'The Lisbon Earthquake; Or an Inquiry into the Maxim, "Whatever Is, Is Again Right"', in *Candide, or Optimism*, trans. Theo Cuffe (London: Penguin, 2005), pp. 100, 106.

6. Jean-Jacques Rousseau, Letter to Voltaire (1756), cited in Mark Molesky, *This Gulf of Fire: The Great Lisbon Earthquake, or Apocalypse in the Age of Science and Reason* (New York: Vintage Books, 2015), p. 331.

7. Ibid., pp. 332–3.

8. Walter Benjamin, 'The Lisbon Earthquake', in *Selected Writings*, vol. 2, part 2, *1931–1934*, trans. Rodney Livingstone et al. (Cambridge, MA: Belknap Press of Harvard University Press, 1999), pp. 537–8.

9. Kant was born in 1724, and would therefore have been thirty-one at the time of the earthquake.

10. Benjamin, 'The Lisbon Earthquake', p. 538.

11. Immanuel Kant, 'On the Causes of Earthquakes on the Occasion of the Calamity That Befell the Western Countries of Europe towards the End of Last Year', 'History and Natural Description of the Most Noteworthy Occurrences of the Earthquake That Struck a Large Part of the Earth at the End of the Year 1755', 'Continued Observations on the Earthquakes That

Have Been Experienced for Some Time', trans. Olaf Reinhardt, in *Natural Science*, ed. Eric Watkins (Cambridge: Cambridge University Press, 2012), pp. 327–73.

12. Ibid., pp. 333, 358, 360.

13. Ibid., p. 363.

14. We might put the point in more explicitly Lacanian terms and say that 'Lisbon' is the missing signifier in Kant's theory of the sublime. It is interesting also to note that, according to Susan Neiman's classic study, the modern problem of evil begins with Lisbon: 'The eighteenth century used the word *Lisbon* much as we use the word *Auschwitz* today.' Susan Neiman, *Evil in Modern Thought: An Alternative History of Philosophy* (Princeton, NJ: Princeton University Press, 2015), p. 1.

15. The classic study here is Arthur O. Lovejoy, *The Great Chain of Being: A Study of the History of an Idea* (Cambridge, MA: Harvard University Press, 2001).

16. Benjamin Stillingfleet, *Saturday Magazine*, 7 January 1837.

17. George Lakoff and Mark Turner, *More than Cool Reason: A Field Guide to Poetic Metaphor* (Chicago: University of Chicago Press, 1989), p. 167.

18. Georges Cuvier, 'Espèces des éléphans' (Species of Elephants, 1796), in Martin J. S. Rudwick, *Georges Cuvier, Fossil Bones, and Geological Catastrophes* (Chicago: University of Chicago Press, 1997), p. 24.

19. Georges Cuvier, *Essay on the Theory of the Earth*, trans. Robert Kerr (Cambridge: Cambridge University Press, 2009), pp. 16–17.

20. Ibid., p. 3.

21. Paul Valéry, 'The Crisis of the Mind', in *Paul Valéry: An Anthology* (London: Routledge & Kegan Paul, 1977), p. 94.

22. We should note here that Kant's work on the sublime stands in a long tradition of aesthetic speculation. After Boileau's 1674 translation of Longinus, the sublime assumes an important

philosophical role and is discussed by Burke, Herder, and Mendelssohn, before Kant, and by an eclectic range of figures – including Hegel, Schopenhauer, Nietzsche, Lacan, Lyotard, Derrida, Kristeva, and Jameson – after him.

23. Immanuel Kant, *Critique of Judgement*, trans. Werner S. Pluhar (Cambridge, MA: Hackett, 1987), p. 115.

24. Kant, 'History and Natural Description', p. 340.

25. Kant, *Critique of Judgement*, p. 120.

26. Ibid., pp. 98–9.

27. Ibid., p. 121.

28. See, for example, Donald Pease, 'Sublime Politics', in *The American Sublime*, ed. Mary Arensberg (Albany: State University of New York Press, 1991). That violence and domination are the key features of the Kantian sublime is also a claim made by a number of left-wing readers of the third *Critique*. See, for example, Tom Huhn, 'The Kantian Sublime and the Nostalgia for Violence', *Journal of Aesthetics and Art Criticism* 53(3), 1995, pp. 269–75.

29. Ernst Bloch, ' "Entfremdung, Verfremdung": Alienation, Estrangement', *Drama Review: TDR* 15(1), 1970, pp. 120–5 (125).

30. Immanuel Kant, 'The Contest of Faculties', in *Kant: Political Writings*, trans. H. B. Nisbet (Cambridge: Cambridge University Press, 1991), p. 182.

31. Ibid.

32. Ibid., pp. 182–3.

33. Immanuel Kant, *The Metaphysics of Morals*, trans. Mary Gregor (Cambridge: Cambridge University Press, 2013), pp. 96–8.

34. Freud, 'Fetishism', *SE* 21, p. 153.

35. See Immanuel Kant, *Religion within the Boundaries of Mere Reason and Other Writings*, trans. Allen Wood (Cambridge: Cambridge University Press, 1998), p. 68.

36. Immanuel Kant, 'An Answer to the Question: "What Is Enlightenment?"', in *Kant: Political Writings*, p. 55.

37. Marquis de Sade, *Juliette*, trans. Austryn Wainhouse (New York: Arrow Books, 1991), p. 767.

38. Ibid., p. 768.

39. Ibid., p. 771.

40. Theodor Adorno and Max Horkheimer, *Dialectic of Enlightenment*, trans. John Cumming (London: Verso, 1997), pp. 94–5.

41. Sade, *Juliette*, p. 771.

42. Ibid., p. 782.

43. Jacques Lacan, *The Seminar of Jacques Lacan, Book XVII: The Other Side of Psychoanalysis*, trans. Russell Grigg (London: W. W. Norton & Co., 1991), p. 67.

44. Slavoj Žižek, *Disparities* (London: Bloomsbury, 2016), p. 335.

45. Ibid.

46. Gustav Metzger, *Writings 1953–2016*, ed. Matthew Copeland (Geneva: JRP Editions, 2019), p. 615.

47. See Max Liljefors, Gregor Noll, and Daniel Steuer, *War and Algorithm* (London: Rowman & Littlefield, 2019).

48. Khari Johnson, 'The US Military, Algorithmic Warfare, and Big Tech', *Venture Beat*, 8 November 2019.

49. Sade, *Juliette*, p. 525.

50. A report published in 2019 found that the US Department of Defense is the world's largest producer of greenhouse gases, with the ongoing war on terror accounting for about 35 per cent of its total carbon emissions. In a darkly comic twist, the US military is now scrambling to protect its bases and radar systems from the climate heating and ecological destruction for which it itself is partly to blame. The 2017 National Authorization Act, signed by US president Donald Trump, points out that 128 military bases would be at risk following a three-foot rise in sea level. According to the same bill: 'In the Arctic, the combination of melting sea ice, thawing permafrost, and

sea-level rise is eroding shorelines, which is damaging radar and communication installations, runways, seawalls, and training areas ... In the Marshall Islands, an Air Force radar installation built on an atoll at a cost of $1,000,000,000 is projected to be underwater within two decades.'

51. It would be incorrect to think of the production of these images as 'random' acts of violence. As Seymour Hersh notes, in discussions among neo-con war strategists prior to the invasion of Iraq, two themes emerged as talking points: (1) 'Arabs only understand force'; (2) the 'biggest weakness of Arabs is shame and humiliation'. Seymour Hersh, 'The Gray Zone', *New Yorker*, 24 May 2004.

52. Stanley Cavell, *Must We Mean What We Say?* (Cambridge: Cambridge University Press, 2003), p. 286.

53. Joan Copjec, 'The Object Gaze: Shame, *Hejab*, Cinema', *Gramma: A Journal of Theory and Criticism* 14, 2006, pp. 163–82 (179).

54. Lacan sees a new culture of *shamelessness* being produced by capitalism. In his Seminar XVII, he argues that shame, as that mode of affect which regulates social bonds, proscribing certain limits to *jouissance*, is precisely what evaporates under contemporary capitalism: 'you can say that there is no longer any shame.' Lacan, *Seminar XVII*, pp. 180–3.

55. Walter Benjamin, *The Arcades Project*, trans. Howard Eiland and Kevin McLaughlin (Cambridge, MA: Harvard University Press, 1999), p. 462 (N2a, 3).

56. Adorno comments that the 'natural catastrophe' of the Lisbon earthquake was nothing when compared to the catastrophe 'we face today – when socially produced evil has engendered something like a real hell'. See Theodor W. Adorno, *Metaphysics: Concept and Problems*, trans. Edmund Jephcott (London: Polity Press, 2001), p. 105.

57. Kant, *Religion within the Boundaries of Mere Reason and Other Writings*, pp. 52 and 54.

58. Ibid., p. 56.

59. Ibid., p. 58.

60. Lacan's reading here faithfully follows (without acknowledging it) Hegel's famous critique of Kant's 'empty formalism'. Jacques Lacan, 'Kant avec Sade', in *Écrits*, trans. Bruce Fink (New York: W. W. Norton & Co., 2006), pp. 345–68. For Hegel, Kant's ethics 'cling[s] ... to a merely moral point of view', and consequently offers little beyond 'an empty formalism' or 'an empty rhetoric of duty for duty's sake'. It fails to make the transition from 'universal' to 'particular'. The categorical imperative would, Hegel argues, be all 'very well if we already had determinate principles concerning how to act'; however, Kant's principle is 'defective' precisely because it has to either smuggle in a set of cultural presuppositions 'from outside' (for example, 'property and human life should exist and be respected'), or it has to proceed on a purely formal basis, in which case 'there is no criterion within [the] principle for deciding whether or not this [or that particular] content is a duty. On the contrary it is possible to justify any wrong or immoral mode of action by this means.' G. W. F. Hegel, *Elements of the Philosophy of Right*, trans. H. B. Nisbet (Cambridge: Cambridge University Press, 2012), §§133–5. What Lacan fails to see is that his own ethical maxim from his Seminar VII – *do not give way in relation to your desire* – is in essence a libertarian version of Kant's categorical imperative. *Do not give way in relation to one's desire for what, exactly?*, we might ask.

61. I have argued elsewhere that Kant's formula is indeed radical. See Ben Ware, *Living Wrong Life Rightly* (London: Palgrave, 2017), ch. 5. However, under capitalism, Kant's 'never simply as a means' is ruled out *a priori*: for the money-owner the possessor of labour power can *only ever* be a mere means. The full realization of Kant's formula would thus require precisely the kind of revolutionary political transformation that his philosophy elsewhere rules out.

62. For a general historical overview of the demonic, see Jeffrey Burton Russell, *Mephistopheles: The Devil in the Modern World* (Ithaca, NY: Cornell University Press, 1990). For an eclectic contemporary assessment, which leans towards psychoanalysis, see Laurence A. Rickels, *The Devil Notebooks* (London: University of Minnesota Press, 2005).

63. For an excellent short assessment of evil, which touches on the demonic, see Terry Eagleton, *On Evil* (New Haven, CT: Yale University Press, 2010).

64. Jean-Paul Sartre, *Saint Genet: Actor and Martyr*, trans. Bernard Frechtman (London: University of Minnesota Press, 2012), p. 235.

65. Here I paraphrase Jacques Lacan, who in the final session of his Seminar XI remarks: '*I love you, but, because inexplicably I love in you something more than you – the* objet petit a *– I mutilate you.*' See Jacques Lacan, *The Seminar of Jacques Lacan, Book XI: The Four Fundamental Concepts of Psychoanalysis*, trans. Alan Sheridan (New York: W. W. Norton & Co., 1981), p. 263.

66. Søren Kierkegaard, *The Concept of Anxiety*, trans. Reidar Thomte and Albert B. Anderson (Princeton, NJ: Princeton University Press, 1980), p. 133.

67. Walter Benjamin, 'Capitalism as Religion', in *Selected Writings*, vol. 1, *1913–1926* (Cambridge, MA: Belknap Press of Harvard University Press, 2004), pp. 288–9. In the following discussion of demonic capitalism, I deliberately avoid focusing on the work of the existential philosopher and theologian Paul Tillich. Tillich found capitalism to be 'demonic' in two key respects. First, it subjects all spheres of life to itself, and deprives things of their essential meaning. Second, 'it causes class struggle and other destructive divisions in society'. But this account is far too simplistic, too moralistic, and too undialectical to be of any real interest. Tillich also has a tendency to lapse into the tiresome register of *Kulturkritik*. For Tillich capitalism produces

the 'mechanised masses' who support the system; it also monopolizes our time leaving a 'lack of time for contemplating the eternal'. See Francis Ching Wah Yip, *Capitalism as Religion: A Study of Paul Tillich's Interpretation of Modernity* (Cambridge, MA: Harvard University Press, 2010), pp. 32–3.

68. The German word *Schuld/Schulden* (used by Benjamin in the original version of his text) means both debt and guilt.

69. Benjamin, 'Capitalism as Religion', p. 288.

70. See Lacan, *Seminar XI*, pp. 212–13.

71. Friedrich Nietzsche, *On the Genealogy of Morality*, trans. Carol Diethe (Cambridge: Cambridge University Press, 2013), ch. 2 ('The Second Essay: "Guilt", "Bad Conscience" and Related Matters'). For an insightful reading of Nietzsche's text in relation to debt/guilt, see Howard Caygill, 'Debt and the Origins of Obedience', in *Force and Understanding: Writings on Philosophy and Resistance* (London: Bloomsbury, 2020), pp. 419–29.

72. There is a clear and obvious parallel here with our debt to the superego: the more sacrifices we make to it, the more it demands. Specifically in the case of the obsessional neurotic, the superego's demands are cruel and relentless; there is never a point when enough is *enough*.

73. On *Squid Game* as a critique of capitalism, see Caitlyn Clark, 'Squid Game Is an Allegory of Capitalist Hell', *Jacobin*, 10 June 2021. It is worth bearing in mind that the show's creator, Hwang Dong-hyuk, explicitly said that he 'wanted to write a story that was an allegory or fable about modern capitalist society'. It seems he didn't know quite how well he had succeeded: one of the things that modern capitalism demonstrates is a remarkable ability for self-reproduction through ostensibly 'anti-capitalist' culture.

74. Benjamin, 'Capitalism as Religion', p. 288.

75. Kierkegaard, *The Concept of Anxiety*, pp. 118ff.

76. Lacan, *Seminar XVII*, p. 208.

77. Karl Marx, *Capital: A Critique of Political Economy*, vol. 1, trans. Ben Fowkes (London: Penguin, 1990), p. 742.

78. Ibid., pp. 254–5.

79. Ibid., p. 1007.

80. Ibid., pp. 279–80.

81. Ibid., p. 356.

82. Ibid., pp. 482 and 416.

83. Ibid., p. 503.

84. Ibid., p. 926.

85. Karl Marx, 'A Contribution to the Critique of Hegel's Philosophy of Right: Introduction', in *Marx: Early Political Writings*, trans. Joseph O'Malley (Cambridge: Cambridge University Press, 1994), p. 69.

86. Ibid.

87. Ibid.

88. See Terry Eagleton, 'Tragedy and Revolution', in *Theology and the Political: New Debates*, ed. Creston Davis et al. (Durham, NC: Duke University Press, 2005), p. 12.

89. Sophocles, 'Oedipus at Colonus', in *The Theban Plays*, trans. E. F. Watling (London: Penguin, 1947), p. 83.

3 The Death Drive at the End of the World

1. Freud, 'On Transience', *SE* 14, p. 305.

2. Ibid.

3. Ibid., p. 306.

4. See Matthew von Unwerth, *Freud's Requiem: Mourning, Memory, and the Invisible History of a Summer Walk* (London: Bloomsbury, 2005).

5. Ibid.

6. Jonathan Lear, 'Transience and Hope: A Return to Freud in a Time of Pandemic', *International Journal of Psychoanalysis* 102, 2021, pp. 3–15.

7. Freud, 'On Transience', p. 307.

8. Here one is reminded of the political slogan used by Joe Biden in his 2020 US presidential campaign: 'Build Back Better'. This was also the name of Bill Clinton's 'humanitarian' programme in Haiti; and in 2021 it was the name of the UK government's plan for 'post-Brexit growth'.

9. Theodor Adorno, *Minima Moralia: Reflections from Damaged Life*, trans. E. F. N. Jephcott (London: Verso, 2002), p. 55.

10. Giorgio Agamben, *Stanzas: Words and Phantasm in Western Culture*, trans. Robert L. Martinez (Minneapolis: University of Minnesota Press, 1993), p. 20.

11. Rosa Luxemburg, 'The Junius Pamphlet, Pt. 1: The Crisis in German Social Democracy', in *Selected Political Writings of Rosa Luxemburg*, ed. Dick Howard (New York: Monthly Review Press, 1971), p. 324. For Lenin's critical comments on the pamphlet, see V. I. Lenin, 'Junius Pamphlet', *Sbornik Sotsial-Demokrata* 1, October 1916.

12. Freud, 'On Transience', p. 305.

13. See Rainer Maria Rilke, *The Notebooks of Malte Laurids Brigge*, trans. M. D. Herter Norton (New York: W. W. Norton & Co., 1992), p. 18.

14. Rainer Maria Rilke, *Selected Poems*, trans. J. B. Leishman (London: Penguin, 1964), p. 63. Rilke was profoundly affected by a change in the status of objects at the beginning of the twentieth century, and specifically their transformation into commodities. As Agamben notes: 'in a letter of 1912, Rilke wrote of the change that had come over things in terms that closely recall Marx's analysis of the fetishistic character of the commodity. "The world contracts", Rilke writes, "because even things, for their part, do the same, in that they continuously displace their existence into the vibration of money, developing a kind of spirituality that from this moment on outstrips the tangible reality."' Agamben, *Stanzas*, p. 38.

15. Freud, 'On Transience', pp. 306, 307.

16. On this connection, see David Bennett, '"Money Is Laughing Gas to Me" (Freud): A Critique of Pure Reason in Economics and Psychoanalysis', *New Formations* 72, 2011, pp. 5–18; David Bennett, 'Desire as Capital: Getting a Return on the Repressed Libidinal Economy', in *Metaphors of Economy*, ed. Nicole Bracker and Stefan Herbrechter (Amsterdam: Rodopi, 2005), pp. 95–112; Lawrence Birkin, 'Freud's "Economic Hypothesis": From Homo Oeconomicus to Homo Sexualis', *American Imago* 56(4), 1999, pp. 311–30; Jean-Joseph Goux, 'Pleasure and Pain: At the Crossroads of Psychoanalysis and the Political Economy', *New Formations* 72, 2011, pp. 117–28. For an early suggestion of this connection, see Marc Shell, 'The Money Complex in Psychoanalysis', in *Money, Language, and Thought* (Baltimore, MD: Johns Hopkins University Press, 1982), pp. 196–9. Also important here is Gilles Deleuze's claim that 'there is only one economy, not two; and desire or libido is just the subjectivity of political economy'. See Gilles Deleuze, 'Preface: Three Group Related Problems', in Félix Guattari, *Psychoanalysis and Transversality: Texts and Interviews 1955– 1971*, trans. Ames Hodges (South Pasadena, CA: Semiotext(e), 2015), p. 10. One might argue that psychoanalysis itself turns out to be worse than capitalism. Under capitalism, the worker sells their labour power in return for a wage; in psychoanalysis, by contrast, the analysand pays to go to work. For an illuminating exploration of this point, see Dany Nobus, 'What Are Words Worth? Lacan and the Circulation of Money in the Psychoanalytic Economy', in *Critique of Psychoanalytic Reason: Studies in Lacanian Theory and Practice* (London: Routledge, 2022), ch. 2.

17. See J. S. Mill, 'On the Definition of Political Economy; and the Method of Investigation Proper to It', in *Essays on Some Unsettled Questions in Political Economy* (London: Longmans,

1874); reprinted in J. S. Mill, *Collected Works*, vol. 4 (Toronto: Toronto University Press, 1967), pp. 120–64.

18. Freud, 'On Transience', pp. 306–7.

19. Freud, 'Mourning and Melancholia', *SE* 14, p. 245.

20. Elizabeth Roudinesco, *Freud: In His Time and Ours*, trans. Catherine Porter (Cambridge, MA: Harvard University Press, 2016), p. 203.

21. Freud, Letter to Binswanger, 12 April 1929, in *The Sigmund Freud–Ludwig Binswanger Correspondence, 1908–1938*, ed. Gerhard Fichtner (London: Open Court Press, 2003), p. 196.

22. The notion of authentic or resolute 'being-towards-death' is, of course, the cornerstone of Heidegger's ethics. See Martin Heidegger, *Being and Time*, trans. John Macquarrie and Edward Robinson (Oxford: Blackwell, 2000), §§235–67. Heidegger's connection to Freud and Freudianism is little commented upon, although the texts contained in the so-called *Zollikon Seminars* bring an intriguing, though hostile, relation to light. According to the Swiss psychiatrist Medard Boss, who introduced Heidegger to Freud's work, and who had himself been analysed by Freud in the 1920s: 'During his perusal of the theoretical, "metapsychological" works, Heidegger never ceased shaking his head. He simply did not want to have to accept that such a highly intelligent and gifted man as Freud could produce such artificial, inhuman, indeed absurd, and purely fictitious constructions about *homo sapiens*. This reading made him literally feel ill.' See Martin Heidegger, *Zollikon Seminars: Protocols–Conversations–Letters*, ed. Medard Boss (Evanston, IL: Northwestern University Press, 2001), p. 309.

23. See Jacques Lacan, *The Seminar of Jacques Lacan, Book VI: Desire and Its Interpretation*, trans. Bruce Fink (London: Polity, 2019), p. 336.

24. Freud, 'Beyond the Pleasure Principle', *SE* 18, p. 9.

25. Ibid., p. 35.

26. James Strachey incorrectly translates *Trieb* as 'instinct', and not 'drive', in Freud's work. There is no *death instinct* in Freud. Each time the word 'instinct' appears we should re-translate it as 'drive'.

27. Freud, 'Beyond the Pleasure Principle', pp. 36, 38.

28. It should be pointed out that the Helmholtz School, to which Freud was heir, had as its specific objective the application of the physical laws of thermodynamics to the study of living organisms. Freud's supervisor at the University of Vienna, Wilhelm von Brücke, proposed the concept of *psychodynamics*, which was rooted in the principles of thermodynamics. According to Brücke, all living organisms are in fact energy systems analogous to non-living (closed) systems with respect to thermodynamic laws. Freud's early work moves in this direction. See, specifically, his 'Project for a Scientific Psychology', *SE* 1, pp. 281–343. The 'Project' provides the groundwork for the later notion of *Todestrieb*.

29. Cited in P. M. Harman, *Energy, Force, and Matter: The Conceptual Developments of Nineteenth-Century Physics* (London: Cambridge University Press, 1982), p. 65.

30. See Ilya Prigogine and Isabelle Stengers, *Order out of Chaos: Man's New Dialogue with Nature* (London: Verso, 2017), p. 119.

31. Cited in Anson Rabinbach, *The Human Motor: Energy, Fatigue, and the Origins of Modernity* (Berkeley: University of California Press, 1992), p. 62.

32. Lord Byron, *Poetical Works* (London: Oxford University Press, 1945), p. 95.

33. Claude Lévi-Strauss, *Tristes tropiques*, trans. John Weightman and Doreen Weightman (London: Penguin, 2011), p. 413.

34. Norbert Wiener, *Cybernetics: Or Control and Communication in the Animal and the Machine* (Cambridge, MA: MIT Press, 2013), p. 154.

35. George Caffentzis, *In Letters of Blood and Fire: Work, Machines, and the Crisis of Capitalism* (Oakland, CA: PM Press, 2013), pp. 13, 14, 12.

36. William Thomson, 'On a Universal Tendency in Nature to the Dissipation of Mechanical Energy' (1852), cited in Crosbie Smith and M. Norbert Wise, *Energy and Empire: A Biographical Study of Lord Kelvin* (Cambridge: Cambridge University Press, 1989), pp. 499–500.

37. Engels vehemently rejects this eschatological extension of the Second Law on materialist grounds, without rejecting the entropy principle per se. And indeed, according to much recent scientific work on the topic, he was correct to do so. As Eric Schneider and Dorian Sagan point out: 'Far from predicting cosmic burnout, modern thermodynamics shows how complex structures, living or not, often come into being, expand, and increase their complexity in regions of the universe exposed to energy flow; because the interaction of the fundamental forces of the universe (gravity, electromagnetism, the weak and strong nuclear forces) is not completely integrated, nor the total matter of the universe known, guarantees of a heat death (or even an end) are not scientifically credible.' Eric Schneider and Dorian Sagan, *Into the Cool: Energy Flow, Thermodynamics, and Life* (Chicago: Chicago University Press, 2005), p. 6.

38. Michel Serres, *Hermes: Literature, Science, Philosophy* (Baltimore, MD: The Johns Hopkins University Press, 1982), p. 72. Indeed, in one respect, Freud's biological determinism only really makes sense if applied to a physics model.

39. Louis Althusser, *On Ideology* (London: Verso, 2008), p. 149.

40. See Adrian Johnston, *Time Driven: Metapsychology and the Splitting of the Drive* (Evanston, IL: Northwestern University Press, 2005), p. 183.

41. Ibid.

42. Adrian Johnston, 'The Weakness of Nature: Hegel, Freud, Lacan and the Negativity Materialized', in *Hegel and the Infinite: Religion, Politics and Dialectic*, ed. Slavoj Žižek,

Clayton Crockett, and Creston Davis (New York: Columbia University Press, 2011), p. 160.

43. In this respect, subjectivity is caught up in an irresolvable tension: there is a traumatic kernel that it cannot get rid of, but which it cannot help attempting to get rid of. One of the best contemporary explorations of the death drive in Lacan, and one from which this section has benefited greatly, is Alenka Zupančič's *What Is Sex?* (Cambridge, MA: MIT Press, 2017), ch. 4.

44. Jacques Lacan, *The Seminar of Jacques Lacan, Book XVII: The Other Side of Psychoanalysis*, trans. Russell Grigg (London: W. W. Norton & Co., 1991), p. 45.

45. Stanley Cavell, *Must We Mean What We Say?* (Cambridge: Cambridge University Press, 2003), p. 161.

46. Jacques Lacan, *The Seminar of Jacques Lacan, Book XI: The Four Fundamental Concepts of Psychoanalysis*, trans. Alan Sheridan (New York: W. W. Norton & Co., 1981), p. 61.

47. See Eric Santner, who here draws deliberately on the lyrics of the song made famous by Frank Sinatra and later by the Sex Pistols. Eric L. Santner, *Untying Things Together: Philosophy, Literature, and a Life in Theory* (Chicago: University of Chicago Press, 2022), p. 194.

48. The ideas put forward in Cohle's speech also have clear connections with ideas found in Thomas Ligotti, *The Conspiracy against the Human Race* (London: Penguin, 2018).

49. Sophocles, *Four Tragedies*, trans. Oliver Taplin (Oxford: Oxford University Press, 2015), p. 272. (This is an alternative translation to the one used in the previous chapter as it captures the tragic maxim much more clearly.)

50. Friedrich Nietzsche, *The Birth of Tragedy and Other Writings*, trans. Ronald Spiers (Cambridge: Cambridge University Press, 1999), p. 23.

51. Freud, 'Jokes and Their Relation to the Unconscious', *SE* 8, p. 57.

52. See Bernard Williams, 'The Makropulos Case: Reflections on the Tedium of Immortality', in *Problems of the Self* (Cambridge: Cambridge University Press, 1999), p. 87.

53. Freud, *SE* 8, p. 57.

54. See David Benatar, *Better Never to Have Been: The Harm of Coming into Existence* (Oxford: Oxford University Press, 2008), p. 4.

55. Aaron Schuster, *The Trouble with Pleasure: Deleuze and Psychoanalysis* (Cambridge, MA: MIT Press, 2016), p. 15.

56. This is, in essence, the argument of Benatar's *Better Never to Have Been*. For an overview of anti-natalist arguments, see Ken Coats, *Anti-natalism: Rejectionist Philosophy from Buddhism to Benatar* (Sarasota, FL: Design Publishing, 2014).

57. Arthur Schopenhauer, *Studies in Pessimism*, trans. T. Bailey Saunders (London: Swan Sonnenschein & Co., 1891), p. 14.

58. P. W. Zapffe, 'The Last Messiah', *Philosophy Now* 45, 2004 (translation slightly amended).

59. Arthur Schopenhauer, *The World as Will and Representation*, vol. 2 (Cambridge: Cambridge University Press, 2018), p. 252.

60. 'A Brief History of the Church of Euthanasia', churchofeuthanasia. org.

61. Patricia MacCormack, *The Ahuman Manifesto: Activism for the Age of the Anthropocene* (London: Bloomsbury, 2020), p. 140.

62. Ibid., p. 162.

63. Ibid., p. 141.

64. Ibid., pp. 10, 9.

65. Lee Edelman, *No Future: Queer Theory and the Death Drive* (Durham, NC: Duke University Press, 2004), pp. 2, 3, 11, 4, 75.

66. The figure who embodies this radical negativity is the 'sintho-mosexual': a neologism which Edelman adapts from Lacan's

notion of the *sinthome* – the unanalysable kernel of the subject which binds together the three registers of the real, the imaginary, and the symbolic. See Jacques Lacan, *The Sinthome: The Seminar of Jacques Lacan, Book XXIII* (London: Polity Press, 2016).

67. Edelman, *No Future*, p. 29. It is perhaps not insignificant that Edelman's hostility is, at times, explicitly directed at working-class children, and specifically girls: 'fuck Annie, fuck the waif in *Les Mis*' (29).

68. Thom van Dooren, *Flight Ways: Life and Loss at the Edge of Extinction* (New York: Columbia University Press, 2014), p. 12.

69. Karl Marx and Friedrich Engels, *The Communist Manifesto*, trans. Samuel Moore (London: Penguin, 2002), p. 223.

70. Theodor W. Adorno, *Metaphysics: Concept and Problems*, trans. Edmund Jephcott (London: Polity Press, 2001), p. 106.

71. Ibid., p. 136.

72. James Joyce, *Ulysses* (London: Penguin, 2000), p. 133.

73. W. B. Yeats, 'Calvary', in *The Collected Works of W. B. Yeats*, vol. 2, *The Plays* (New York: Scribner, 2001), p. 336.

74. Ibid., p. 337.

75. Colossal claims: 'We have the DNA, the technology, and the leading experts in the field. Next, we will have the Woolly Mammoth. Alive again.' Colossal founders, George Church and Ben Lamm, have racked up a list of high-profile donors and investors, including Peter Thiel, Paris Hilton, and In-Q-Tel (IQT), the investment arm of the CIA.

76. Colossal Laboratories and Biosciences website, colossal.com.

77. Ross Andersen, 'How Engineering the Human Body Could Combat Climate Change', *Atlantic*, 12 March 2012.

78. George Church and Ed Regis, *Regenesis: How Synthetic Biology Will Reinvent Nature and Ourselves* (New York: Basic Books, 2012), p. 7.

79. Aldo Leopold, *A Sand County Almanac* (Oxford: Oxford University Press, 1949), p. 224.

80. Amy Lynn Fletcher, *Mendel's Ark: Biotechnology and the Future of Extinction* (New York: Springer, 2014), p. 5.

81. Beth Shapiro, *How to Clone a Mammoth: The Science of De-extinction* (Princeton, NJ: Princeton University Press, 2020), p. x. See also Erica Borg and Amedeo Policante, *Mutant Ecologies: Manufacturing Life in the Age of Genomic Capital* (London: Pluto, 2022), ch. 6.

82. It is odd that most people still read the child as throwing the reel *out of his cot,* and not 'into it', as Freud makes very clear, as if the details of Freud's text don't matter.

83. Jonathan Lear, *Happiness, Death, and the Remainder of Life* (Cambridge, MA: Harvard University Press, 2000), pp. 92, 94.

84. Ibid., p. 94.

85. Freud, 'The "Uncanny"', *SE* 17, p. 235.

86. Cited in Susan Buck-Morss, *The Dialectics of Seeing: Walter Benjamin and the 'Arcades Project'* (Cambridge, MA: MIT Press, 1999), p. 101.

87. Jean Baudrillard, *Passwords* (London: Verso, 2003), p. 66.

88. Max More, 'A Letter to Mother Nature', in *The Transhumanist Reader: Classical and Contemporary Essays on the Science, Technology, and Philosophy of the Human Future*, ed. Max More and Natasha Vita-More (Oxford: John Wiley & Sons, 2013), p. 450.

89. Cited in Anastasia Gacheva, 'Art as the Overcoming of Death: From Nikolai Fedorov to the Cosmists of the 1920s', *e-flux journal* 89, 2018. On Fedorov and the Cosmists, see George M. Young, *The Russian Cosmists: Nikolai Fedorov and His Esoteric Followers* (Oxford: Oxford University Press, 2012); Anya Bernstein, *The Future of Immortality: Remaking Life and Death in Contemporary Russia* (Princeton, NJ:

Princeton University Press, 2019); *Russian Cosmism*, ed. Boris Groys (Cambridge, MA: e-flux/MIT Press, 2018).

90. Alexander Svyatogor, 'Our Affirmations', in *Russian Cosmism*, p. 60.

91. Ibid.

92. Jacob Banas, 'Disrupting the Reaper', *Futurism*, 10 December 2018, at futurism.com.

93. Maya Kosoff, 'Peter Thiel Wants to Inject Himself with Other People's Blood', *Vanity Fair*, 1 August 2016; Jeff Bercovici, 'Peter Thiel Is Very, Very Interested in Young People's Blood', *Inc.*, 1 August 2016; Bernstein, *The Future of Immortality*, p. 78.

94. Anthony Cuthbertson, 'Billionaire Trump Supporter Peter Thiel Denies Being a Vampire', *Independent*, 2 November 2018.

95. Freud, 'Negation', *SE* 19, pp. 235–9. Freud begins the essay by discussing the manner in which patients bring forward their associations in analysis. When the patient insists, ' "this person in the dream . . . it's *not* my mother" ', Freud says we can 'emend this to: "So it *is* his mother." In our interpretation, we take the liberty of disregarding the negation and of picking out the subject-matter alone of the association.'

96. Alexander Bogdanov, 'Immortality Day', in *Russian Cosmism*, pp. 215–26. Bogdanov was a key figure within the Russian Social Democratic Labour Party and its Bolshevik faction. He was a rival of Lenin, and was expelled from the Bolsheviks in 1909, establishing his own faction, Vpered.

97. Ibid., pp. 215–24.

98. Freud, 'Thoughts for the Times on War and Death', *SE* 14, p. 289.

99. Ibid., p. 298.

100. Ibid., p. 296. In the case of strangers and enemies, by contrast, we do acknowledge death; indeed, in our unconscious 'we daily and hourly get rid of anyone who stands in our way, of

anyone who has offended or injured us ... Our unconscious will murder even for trifles; like the ancient Athenian code of Draco, it knows of no other punishment for crime than death' (297).

101. This psychical antinomy corresponds to the first of Kant's four antinomies in the *Critique of Pure Reason*. In this first, or quantitative antinomy, Kant sets the *thesis* that 'the world has a beginning in time, and is also limited as regards space', alongside the *antithetical* claim that 'the world has no beginning, and no limits in space; it is infinite as regards both time and space'. See Immanuel Kant, *Critique of Pure Reason*, trans. Norman Kemp Smith (London: Palgrave, 2003), p. 396.

102. Slavoj Žižek, '*Da capo senza fine*', in Judith Butler et al., *Contingency, Hegemony, Universality* (London: Verso, 2000), p. 256. See also Adrian Johnston, *Žižek's Ontology: A Transcendental Materialist Theory of Subjectivity* (Evanston, IL: Northwestern University Press, 2008), ch. 3.

103. Immanuel Kant, *Anthropology from a Pragmatic Point of View*, trans. Robert B. Louden (Cambridge: Cambridge University Press, 2006), p. 60.

104. On the connection between immortal, indestructible life and the death drive, see Lacan, *Seminar XI*, esp. ch. 15.

105. Adorno, *Metaphysics: Concept and Problems*, p. 135.

106. Marcel Proust, 'The Captive', in *Remembrance of Things Past*, vol. 3, trans. C. K. Scott Moncrieff and Terence Kilmartin (New York: Random House, 1981), p. 186.

107. Claude Lefort, 'The Death of Immortality?', in *Democracy and Political Theory*, trans. David Macey (London: Polity Press, 1988), p. 267.

108. Ibid., p. 270.

109. Ibid., pp. 270–1.

110. Herbert Marcuse, *Psychoanalysis, Politics, Utopia: Five Lectures* (London: Repeater Books, 2022), p. 83.

111. Jacques Lacan, *The Seminar of Jacques Lacan, Book VII: The Ethics of Psychoanalysis, 1959–1960*, trans. Dennis Porter (London: Routledge, 2008), p. 262.

4 Beginning Again at the End

1. Franz Kafka, *Letters to Friends, Family, and Editors* (London: John Calder, 1978), p. 102.

2. Exactly how many Hunter Gracchus texts there are remains a matter of some debate. In his diary entry for 6 April 1917, Kafka sketches a fragment in which a narrator describes a 'tiny harbor' where a 'strange boat lay at anchor'. The boat is identified as belonging 'to the Hunter Gracchus'. Franz Kafka, *Diaries: 1910–1923*, ed. Max Brod (New York: Schocken Books, 1949), p. 373. This is clearly the germ of the two famous Hunter Gracchus texts. But there is also the germ of this germ in his diary entry for 21 October 1913, written shortly after Kafka returned from his stay at Riva (p. 234). I draw here on the two *key texts* contained in *The Complete Stories*.

3. Franz Kafka, 'The Hunter Gracchus', in *Franz Kafka: The Complete Stories* (New York: Schocken Books, 1971), p. 226.

4. Ibid., p. 227.

5. Ibid., p. 228.

6. John Zilcosky, *Kafka's Travels: Exoticism, Colonialism, and the Traffic of Writing* (London: Palgrave, 2003), p. 185. For an excellent philosophical study of Kafka, which explores the writer's early, middle, and later works, see Howard Caygill, *Kafka: In Light of the Accident* (London: Bloomsbury, 2017).

7. Theodor W. Adorno, 'Notes on Kafka', in *Prisms*, trans. Samuel and Shierry Weber (Cambridge, MA: MIT Press, 1996), p. 260. Adorno also goes on to say that 'Gracchus is

the consummate refutation of the possibility banished from the world: to die after a long and full life' (ibid.). On this point, see also Theodor Adorno, *Minima Moralia: Reflections from Damaged Life*, trans. E. F. N. Jephcott (London: Verso, 2002), pp. 231–3.

8. Theodor W. Adorno, 'Commitment', in *Notes to Literature*, vol. 2, trans. Shierry Weber Nicholsen (New York: Columbia University Press, 1992), p. 94.

9. Kafka, 'The Hunter Gracchus', p. 229.

10. See Jacques Lacan, *The Seminar of Jacques Lacan, Book VII: The Ethics of Psychoanalysis, 1959–1960*, trans. Dennis Porter (London: Routledge, 2008), pp. 299–348.

11. Sophocles, 'Antigone', in *The Theban Plays*, trans. E. F. Watling (London: Penguin, 1947), pp. 148–9.

12. Ibid., p. 150. For a highly insightful reading of Antigone's justification for her act of rebellion, see Alenka Zupančič, *Let Them Rot: Antigone's Parallax* (New York: Fordham University Press, 2023), ch. 3.

13. Kafka, 'The Hunter Gracchus', p. 229.

14. Ibid., p. 230.

15. Ibid., pp. 228–30.

16. Søren Kierkegaard, *The Sickness unto Death*, trans. Howard V. Hong and Edna H. Hong (Princeton, NJ: Princeton University Press, 1980), p. 18.

17. Kafka, 'The Hunter Gracchus', p. 233.

18. Kierkegaard, *The Sickness unto Death*, p. 26.

19. Here I refer to the Alastair Hannay translation. Søren Kierkegaard, *The Sickness unto Death* (London: Penguin, 2004), p. 91.

20. Kierkegaard, *The Sickness unto Death*, p. 44 (Hong translation). For a compelling account of Kierkegaard's notion of despair, see Michael Theunissen, *Kierkegaard's Concept of Despair*, trans. Barbara Harshaw and Helmut Illbruck (Princeton, NJ:

Princeton University Press, 2005). Theunissen's text does a good job of connecting Kierkegaard's philosophy to Hegel's *Phenomenology* and Marx's dialectical materialism.

21. Theodor Adorno, *Negative Dialectics*, trans. E. B. Ashton (London: Routledge, 2004), p. 373.

22. See Fredric Jameson, 'Marx's Purloined Letter', in *Valences of the Dialectic* (London: Verso, 2009), p. 143.

23. Adorno, *Negative Dialectics*, pp. 377–8. The notion of dialectical despair that I advance in these paragraphs deliberately sets itself against what Benjamin describes (in his essay on Erich Kästner's poetry) as the kind of stance that wishes 'to enjoy itself in its negativistic quiet'. See Walter Benjamin, 'Left-Wing Melancholy', in *Selected Writings*, vol. 2, part 2, *1931–1934*, trans. Rodney Livingstone et al (Cambridge, MA: Belknap Press of Harvard University Press, 2005), p. 425. On the contrary, dialectical despair is a precursor to real struggle. Dialectical despair assembles the reminder that the current course of the world is not final, nor is despair itself absolute.

24. Here I push further with Benjamin's final line in his essay on Goethe's *Elective Affinities*: 'Only for the sake of the hopeless ones have we been given hope.' Walter Benjamin, 'Goethe's *Elective Affinities*', in *Selected Writings*, vol. 1, *1913–1926* (Cambridge, MA: Belknap Press of Harvard University Press, 2004), p. 356.

25. Frank Kermode, 'Waiting for the End', in *Apocalypse Theory and the Ends of the World*, ed. Malcolm Bull (London: Blackwell, 1995), p. 250.

26. Frank Kermode, *The Sense of an Ending* (Oxford: Oxford University Press, 2000), p. 192.

27. Eric Cazdyn, *The Already Dead: The New Time of Politics, Culture, and Illness* (Durham, NC: Duke University Press, 2012), pp. 13 and 5.

28. Fredric Jameson, *A Singular Modernity: An Essay on the Ontology of the Present* (London: Verso, 2002), p. 79.

29. Fredric Jameson, 'The End of Temporality' (2003), in *The Ideologies of Theory* (London: Verso, 2008), pp. 643–4.

30. I adapt the phrase 'time loses its flow' from Denise Riley, *Time Lived without Its Flow* (London: Picador, 2012). Riley's book is an immensely powerful and deeply moving account of personal loss. On the issue of limbo: it is interesting to observe that at the very start of the current crisis period (the global financial collapse that began in 2007), Pope Benedict XVI signed a report effectively cancelling the (theological) idea of limbo. See Ian Fisher, 'Pope Closes Limbo', *New York Times*, 21 April 2007.

31. For a discussion of the temporality of presentism, see François Hartog, *Regimes of Historicity: Presentism and Time*, trans. Saskia Brown (New York: Columbia University Press, 2015).

32. The term *depression* is, of course, not unproblematic. Lacan himself takes a strong line, saying that 'we qualify sadness as depression, because we give it soul for support . . . But it isn't a state of the soul, it is simply a moral failing, as Dante, and even Spinoza, said: a sin, which means a moral weakness.' Jacques Lacan, *Television: A Challenge to the Psychoanalytic Establishment*, trans. Jeffrey Mehlman (New York: W. W. Norton & Co., 1990), p. 22. While this sounds rather harsh, Lacan's point is that depression is based on a rejection of the unconscious. The subject, he argues, has an ethical duty to be 'well spoken', to overcome one's passion for ignorance, and to engage in the talking cure. Here, however, we might conclude that while depression is not necessarily useful as a diagnostic term, it can nevertheless be retained as a descriptive term, naming certain surface features of suffering. This is the way it continues to be used by many psychoanalysts, including many Lacanians.

33. See Ben Ware, 'Excremental Happiness: From Neurotic Hedonism to Dialectical Pessimism', *College Literature: A Journal of*

Critical Literary Studies 45(2), 2018, pp. 198–221; Alenka Zupančič, *The Odd One In: On Comedy* (Cambridge, MA: MIT Press, 2008), p. 5.

34. Ludwig Wittgenstein, *Tractatus logico-philosophicus*, trans. C. K. Ogden (London: Routledge, 1981), p. 185 (6. 43). Translation slightly modified.

35. I take the notion of the *great refusal* from Herbert Marcuse, who in turn acquires it from Alfred North Whitehead. See Herbert Marcuse, *An Essay on Liberation* (London: Allen Lane, 1969).

36. Here I draw on ideas in Serge Leclaire, *A Child Is Being Killed: On Primary Narcissism and the Death Drive* (Stanford, CA: Stanford University Press, 1998), especially ch. 1.

37. The advertising campaign, as we see during Jack's speech at the wedding reception, is based on Bruegel's painting *Land of Cockaigne* (1567). The painting depicts an overstuffed society: a peasant, a clerk, and a soldier laze about on the ground, exhausted by the excess consumption of food and drink. The reference to the wedding reception in *Melancholia* is, of course, clear. However, in Jack's campaign, the three figures in Bruegel's painting are replaced by three extremely thin female models. Here the famished bodies provide another way of thinking about the (social and cultural) *emptiness* of the wedding reception as Von Trier depicts it.

38. This saying has never actually been verified in Luther's writings; however, there can be no doubt that the sentiment expressed is genuinely Lutheran in its tone. See, for example, Jane Strohl, 'Luther's Spiritual Journey', in *The Cambridge Companion to Martin Luther* (Cambridge: Cambridge University Press, 2003), p. 162.

39. While Justine makes repeated efforts to engage her parents, it seems that she knows deep down that they are a lost cause. The mother's New Age, hippy repudiation of all conventions

is just the flip side of the father's drunken lechery and infantilism.

40. The suggestion that Justine might be thought of as melancholic does not, of course, constitute a diagnosis, but rather a line of theoretical thought. While Lacan did not speak at any signifi- cant length about melancholia, some interesting efforts to examine melancholia from a Lacanian perspective are contained in *Lacan on Depression and Melancholia*, ed. Derek Hook and Stijn Vanheule (London: Routledge, 2023); Russell Grigg, 'Melancholia and the Unabandoned Object', in *Lacan on Madness: Madness, Yes You Can't*, ed. Patricia Gherovici and Manya Steinkoler (London: Routledge, 2015), pp. 139–58; and Darian Leader, *The New Black: Mourning, Melancholia, and Depression* (London: Penguin, 2009).

41. For Adorno, coldness is fundamentally a failure of the bour- geois subject: a failure to care, to feel, to experience. Coldness 'comes to terms' all too quickly with suffering. See Adorno, *Minima Moralia*, p. 74.

42. Leclaire, *A Child Is Being Killed*, ch. 1.

43. Theodor Adorno, *Aesthetics*, trans. Wieland Hoban (London: Polity, 2018), pp. 30–1.

44. Malevich's *Black Square* was first displayed at the famous '0–10' exhibition in Petrograd from December 1915 through to January 1916. The painting was hung diagonally in the corner of a room and close to the ceiling in the traditional position of a Russian icon. See Arthur Danto, *After the End of Art: Contemporary Art and the Pale of History* (Princeton, NJ: Princeton University Press, 2014), p. 154.

45. Kazimir Malevich, 'Suprematist Manifesto' (1916), in *100 Artists' Manifestos from the Futurists to the Stuckists*, ed. Alex Danchev (London: Penguin, 2011), p. 122.

46. Ibid., p. 106.

47. Cited in Danto, *After the End of Art*, p. 154.

48. See *The Complete Poems of Emily Dickinson*, ed. Thomas H. Johnson (Boston: Little Brown & Co., 1960), p. 650, no. 1563.

49. Simone Weil, *Gravity and Grace*, trans. Emma Crawford and Mario von der Ruhr (London: Routledge, 2002), p. 33.

50. For a brief biographical summary of Weil and her political commitments, see the 'Introduction' to Simone Weil, 'Meditations on a Corpse', *New Left Review* 111, 2018, pp. 34–40.

51. Weil, *Gravity and Grace*, pp. 34–5.

52. Anne Carson, *Decreation* (London: Jonathan Cape, 2006), p. 179.

53. Jacques Lacan, 'Proposition of 9 October 1967 on the Psychoanalyst of the School' (1967), trans. R. Grigg, *Analysis* 6, 1995, pp. 1–13.

54. Slavoj Žižek, *The Ticklish Subject: The Absent Centre of Political Ontology* (London: Verso, 2008), p. 190.

55. Lacan, *Seminar VII*, p. 373.

56. Karl Marx, 'A Contribution to the Critique of Hegel's Philosophy of Right: Introduction', in *Marx: Early Political Writings* (Cambridge: Cambridge University Press, 1994), p. 69.

57. George Lukács, *History and Class Consciousness: Studies in Marxist Dialectics* (London: Merlin Press, 1971), p. 80 (emphasis in original).

58. Ibid.

59. This is, in brief, Lacan's general view of alienation as it gets reiterated from the early work on the 'Mirror Stage' onwards. However, in *Seminar XI*, Lacan makes a much more specific point about alienation. In chapter 15 of this seminar, Lacan argues that alienation consists in the either/or choice between being and meaning. But this is not a free choice, and either way the subject loses. As Lacan remarks: 'If we choose meaning the subject disappears, it eludes us, it falls into non-meaning. If we choose meaning, the meaning survives only deprived of that part of non-meaning that is, strictly speaking, that which

constitutes in the realization of the subject, the unconscious. In other words, it is in the nature of this meaning, as it emerges in the field of the Other, to be in a large part of its field, eclipsed by the disappearance of being, induced by the very function of the signifier.' Jacques Lacan, *The Seminar of Jacques Lacan, Book XI: The Four Fundamental Concepts of Psychoanalysis*, trans. Alan Sheridan (New York: W. W. Norton & Co., 1981), 211. Simply put, then, if the subject chooses *being*, it loses meaning; if it chooses *meaning*, then being disappears, as it is condemned to alienating meaning coming from the Other. Alienation in Lacan is also explored by Samo Tomšič, *The Capitalist Unconscious: Marx and Lacan* (London: Verso, 2015); Paul Verhaeghe, 'Lacan's Answer to Alienation: Separation', *Crisis and Critique* 6(1), 2019, pp. 264–388; and Slavoj Žižek, *Incontinence of the Void: Economico-Philosophical Spandrels* (Cambridge, MA: MIT Press, 2017), ch. 8.

60. This romantic critique of alienation, which sees socialism as a return of 'man' [*sic*] to his 'essence', can be found, for example, in Marx's *Economic and Political Manuscripts of 1844*, Lukács's *History and Class Consciousness*, and Erich Fromm's *Marx's Concept of Man* (London: Continuum, 2004). It is from these texts that I take the phrases that appear in quotation marks.

61. Lukács, *History and Class Consciousness*, p. 90.

62. While the kinds of neurosis that flourish under capitalism are clearly responses/resistances to that system, I think we can safely say that the basic mode of subjectivity under communism would still be neurotic, given that subjectivity is here being defined as ontologically split, regardless of the political formation in which it finds itself. However, it seems correct that we should also hold open an empty space for certain *categories to come*. That is, yet-to-be-invented psychic categories or structures that an emancipated society might give rise to over time.

63. Fredric Jameson, *The Seeds of Time* (New York: Columbia University Press, 1994), p. 99; Fredric Jameson, *Late Marxism: Adorno, or the Persistence of the Dialectic* (London: Verso, 2007), p. 102.

64. Adorno, *Minima Moralia*, pp. 156–7 (emphasis added). For a discussion of sleep as a vital counter to the psychotic world of non-stop capitalist activity, see Jonathan Crary, *24/7: Late Capitalism and the Ends of Sleep* (London: Verso, 2013). Here, however, we should not fall into the false conception that sleep is simply unburdened rest: in sleep the signifier is still very much at work. It is not for nothing that both Freud and Lacan insist on treating the dream, first and foremost, as a dream-work (*Traumarbeit*). For an important critique of Crary's argument, see Joan Copjec, 'Battle Fatigue: Kiarostami and Capitalism', in *Lacan contra Foucault*, ed. Rohit Goel and Nadia Bou (London: Bloomsbury, 2019).

65. The term 'sad passions' is derived from the work of Spinoza. In his early *Short Treatise*, Spinoza describes 'sadness, despair, envy, fright, and other evil passions' as 'the real hell itself'. In the later *Ethics*, he makes the famous statement: 'by *Joy* I shall understand ... that *passion by which the Mind passes to a greater perfection*. And by *Sadness*, that *passion by which it passes to a lesser perfection*.' See *The Collected Works of Spinoza*, vol. 1, trans. Edwin Curley (Princeton, NJ: Princeton University Press, 1985), pp. 128 and 500–1.

66. Here we might list bitterness, shame, irritation, disgust, contempt, and rage, to name only a handful.

67. It is indeed part of the wonderful strangeness of human subjects that they can, and often do, derive enjoyment from not enjoying; desire unsatisfied desire; hate the other for having something (intelligence, good looks, a mysterious 'x') that they do not possess; love the other for precisely the same reason; repeat what is painful and traumatic (because it is secretly

enjoyable); repeat what is pleasurable (only to find it utterly depressing); get what they 'officially' want only to self-sabotage for reasons unbeknown to themselves; get someone else, or something else, to enjoy on their behalf; or feel utterly alienated in their enjoyment at precisely the point where they enjoy as part of a 'community'.

68. Karl Marx, 'The Eighteenth Brumaire', in *Marx: Later Political Writings*, trans. Terrell Carver (Cambridge: Cambridge University Press, 1996), p. 35.

69. On the political necessity of tarrying with envy, and the sad passions more generally, see Fredric Jameson, 'An American Utopia', in *An American Utopia: Dual Power and the Universal Army* (London: Verso, 2016). I build upon Jameson's analysis in what follows, arriving at what I think is a more robust conclusion, politically and psychoanalytically speaking. In Jameson's utopia, envy is simply allowed to let rip and is elevated 'into a kind of religion' (ibid., p. 89).

70. Here we are reminded of a famous passage in Saint Augustine's *Confessions*, one that is frequently cited by Lacan. The passage reads: 'I have personally watched and studied a jealous baby. He could not yet speak and, pale with jealousy and bitterness, glared at his brother sharing his mother's milk. Who is unaware of this fact of experience?' Saint Augustine, *Confessions*, trans. Henry Chadwick (Oxford: Oxford University Press, 1998), p. 9. This passage refers to jealousy, and Lacan speaks, in his Seminar XX (where this passage is referenced), of 'jealouissance'. See Jacques Lacan, *The Seminar of Jacques Lacan, Book XX: Encore 1972–1973*, trans. Bruce Fink (London: W. W. Norton & Co., 1999), p. 100. However, Augustine's passage might seem to describe envy rather than jealousy. Simply put, in jealousy I have something that is, I feel, encroached upon by the other who threatens to steal it from me; in envy, by contrast, it is the sight of the other enjoying, through something I do not have, that arouses my resentment.

71. Immanuel Kant, *The Metaphysics of Morals*, trans. Mary Gregor (Cambridge: Cambridge University Press, 2013), p. 206. My account of envy here draws on Lacan. For a useful summary, see John Forrester, 'Justice, Envy, and Psychoanalysis', in *Dispatches from the Freud Wars: Psychoanalysis and Its Passions* (London: Harvard University Press, 1997). For an alternative psychoanalytic view of envy, see Melanie Klein, 'Envy and Gratitude', in *Envy and Gratitude and Other Works, 1946–1963* (London: Vintage, 1997). The foundational sociological text on envy is Helmut Schoeck, *Envy: A Theory of Social Behaviour* (New York: Secker & Warburg, 1969). In the tracks of Spinoza, envy is still dominantly seen as a malevolent emotion. See, for example, Gabriel Taylor, *Deadly Vices* (Oxford: Clarendon Press, 2006).

72. Lacan, *Television*, p. 16.

73. Ibid., p. 15. For a superb reading of Lacan's *Television*, see Peter Buse and Robert Lapsley, 'Gaps in Transmission: Reading Lacan's *Télévision*', *Modern Philology* 120(3), 2023, pp. 394–415.

74. Lacan, *Television*, p. 16.

75. Adorno, *Minima Moralia*, p. 26.

76. Benjamin, 'Experience and Poverty', in *Selected Writings*, vol. 2, part 2, pp. 731–2.

77. Ibid., p. 734.

78. Ibid., p. 732. For an important engagement with Benjamin's essay, see Hal Foster, *Brutal Aesthetics* (Princeton, NJ: Princeton University Press, 2019).

79. Benjamin, 'Experience and Poverty', p. 733.

80. Ibid.

81. Walter Benjamin, 'The Destructive Character', in *Selected Writings*, vol. 2, part 2, p. 541. For an excellent engagement with the destructive/interruptive thinking in Benjamin and Brecht, see Benjamin Noys, *Malign Velocities: Acceleration and Capitalism* (Winchester: Zero Books, 2014), ch. 7.

82. Walter Benjamin, 'Central Park', in *Selected Writings*, vol. 4, *1938–1940*, ed. Howard Eiland and Michael Jennings (Cambridge, MA: Belknap Press of Harvard University Press, 2003), pp. 184–5.

83. Louis Althusser, 'Philosophy as a Revolutionary Weapon', in *Lenin and Philosophy and Other Essays*, trans. Ben Brewster (Delhi: Aakar Books, 2006), p. 8.

84. Karl Marx, *Capital: A Critique of Political Economy*, vol. 1, trans. Ben Fowkes (London: Penguin, 1990), p. 301.

85. Ibid.

86. Marx, 'A Contribution to the Critique', p. 61.

87. Walter Benjamin, 'Chaplin in Retrospect', in *Selected Writings*, vol. 2, part 1, p. 244; Walter Benjamin, 'The Author as Producer', in *Selected Writings*, vol. 2, part 2, p. 779 (translation slightly amended).